The People's Bible

ROLAND CAP EHLKE
General Editor

JOHN C. JESKE
Old Testament Editor

JOHN A. TRAPP
Manuscript Editor

Ecclesiastes
Song of Songs

ROLAND CAP EHLKE

NORTHWESTERN PUBLISHING HOUSE
Milwaukee, Wisconsin

The cover and most of the interior illustrations were originally executed by James Tissot (1836-1902). The illustration of the Jewish bride on page 134 is used by permission of Scripture Union, London, from *The Book of Bible Knowledge*. The photograph of the gazelles at the brook, on page 144, was taken in Israel by Gail Rubin.

Scripture taken from the
HOLY BIBLE, NEW INTERNATIONAL VERSION.
Copyright © 1973, 1978, 1984 International Bible Society.
Used by permission of Zondervan Bible Publishers.

Library of Congress Card 87-62527
Northwestern Publishing House
1250 N. 113th St., P.O. Box 26975, Milwaukee, WI 53226-0975
© 1988 by Northwestern Publishing House.
Published 1988
Printed in the United States of America
ISBN 0-8100-0279-5

CONTENTS

ILLUSTRATIONS

EDITOR'S PREFACE

The People's Bible is just what the name implies — a Bible for the people. It includes the complete text of the Holy Scriptures in the popular New International Version. The commentary following the Scripture sections contains personal applications as well as historical background and explanations of the text.

The authors of *The People's Bible* are men of scholarship and practical insight, gained from years of experience in the teaching and preaching ministries. They have tried to avoid the technical jargon which limits so many commentary series to professional Bible scholars.

The most important feature of these books is that they are Christ-centered. Speaking of the Old Testament Scriptures, Jesus himself declared, "These are the Scriptures that testify about me" (John 5:39). Each volume of *The People's Bible* directs our attention to Jesus Christ. He is the center of the entire Bible. He is our only Savior.

The commentaries also have maps, illustrations and archaeological information when appropriate. All the books include running heads to direct the reader to the passage he is looking for.

This commentary series was initiated by the Commission on Christian Literature of the Wisconsin Evangelical Lutheran Synod.

It is our prayer that this endeavor may continue as it began. We dedicate these volumes to the glory of God and to the good of his people.

Roland Cap Ehlke

Solomon and His Harem

ECCLESIASTES
INTRODUCTION

Name and Author

Although the book of Ecclesiastes is part of the Hebrew Old Testament, its name is actually a Greek word. The word Ecclesiastes goes back to an ancient Greek translation of the Old Testament. Ecclesiastes means "Teacher," or "Preacher." It comes from the book's first verse, "The words of the Teacher, ... " The title, then, is a reference to the teacher or preacher whose words make up the book.

The opening verse goes on to tell us who that individual was, " . . . the Teacher, son of David, king in Jerusalem." This of course was King Solomon. From his capital city of Jerusalem Solomon ruled the nation of Israel during its golden age. His reign lasted forty years, 970-931 B.C.

At times Solomon publicly taught or preached to the people, so he calls himself the Teacher. One such occasion was the dedication of the temple. Then, we are told, Solomon addressed "the whole assembly of Israel" which had gathered (1 Kings 8). Perhaps Ecclesiastes was first presented to such an assembly. Maybe it was an after-dinner speech given by the king to the nobility. (The entire book can be read aloud in about forty minutes.) We aren't told the circumstances under which the book came into being.

Whenever or however Solomon first presented the contents of Ecclesiastes, it was sometime late in his life. Jewish tradition recognizes the book as the product of an old man, reflecting on life and preparing to die.

In spite of what the book itself says, most modern scholars reject the Solomonic authorship. This is in keeping with today's tendency to deny the traditional authorship of many books of the Bible. One commentator, for instance, asserts that the author of Ecclesiastes may have lived somewhere between 500 B.C. and A.D. 100!

Such commentators appeal to two main arguments. First, Ecclesiastes contains Aramaic words along with the Hebrew. Ancient Aramaic was a "cousin" language to Hebrew; both belong to the Semitic family. Supposedly Solomon should have written in pure Hebrew. Yet Aramaic was the international language of trade in the ancient world. With his international contacts, it's no more surprising for Solomon to have used some Aramaic, than it is for modern North Americans to know and use some Spanish words in our day. Aramaic, incidentally, was the language Jesus spoke.

Others argue that the book's circumstances and outlook don't seem to square with the life of Solomon. But as we'll see, they fit Solomon's life perfectly. The life of luxury described in Ecclesiastes and the vast experiences of the author certainly point to Solomon.

The inspired book of Ecclesiastes was composed by Solomon the Teacher-King, just as its first verse states.

Place in the Bible

The ancient Jews classified Ecclesiastes among the five "Megilloth" (the word means scrolls). The other four were the Song of Songs, Ruth, Lamentations and Esther. What binds these books together is that they made up the Scripture lessons for five important Jewish festivals: Song of Songs for Passover, Ruth for Pentecost, Lamentations for the commemoration of the Fall of Jerusalem to the Babylonians, Esther for Purim (commemorating Esther's saving the Jewish people from annihilation) and Ecclesiastes for the Feast of Tabernacles (also known as Succoth, Tents or Booths).

Among other things, the Feast of Tabernacles served as the autumn vintage festival. With its somber reminders of death and the foolishness of living for pleasure, Ecclesiastes would help put a damper on the excesses often associated with such a festival. Similarly today's great festivals of Christmas and Easter ought to center on God's Word rather than self-indulgence.

In our English Bible Ecclesiastes is grouped along with Job, Psalms, Proverbs and the Song of Songs. We call these the *poetical books* of the Old Testament.

While we tend to think of poetry in terms of rhythm and rhyme, Old Testament poetry consists of a balance of thoughts more than of words and sounds. Such balance is called parallelism. This means that one line in Hebrew poetry parallels the next. The second part of a verse echoes the idea of the first, contrasts with it, or expands on it. Here are examples of the three basic types of parallelism found in Ecclesiastes:

> The second thought echoes the first:
> "Meaningless! Meaningless!"
>> says the Teacher.
> "Utterly meaningless!
>> Everything is meaningless!" (1:2)

> The second thought contrasts with the first:
> The wise man has eyes in his head,
>> while the fool walks in darkness. (2:14)

> The second thought expands on the first:
> All man's efforts are for his mouth,
>> yet his appetite is never satisfied. (6:7)

Many parts of Ecclesiastes are not written in this poetic form, while a number of the prophets contain large poetical sections. So this classification as poetical is somewhat arbitrary.

At times the Bible's five poetic books are also referred to as the *wisdom literature* of Scripture. They emphasize how we are to live as God's people, and they offer godly wisdom concerning some of life's most complex problems. For example, the book of Job deals with the problem of suffering in the life of a believer. The central theme of the wisdom of Ecclesiastes will take up our attention in the next section.

Outlook and Purpose

The entire Bible is a unified whole. It all points to Jesus Christ. It all presents the law of God and the gospel of his love in Christ. Nevertheless, within this unity there is room for diversity. Some books are historical, others doctrinal. Some books emphasize one theme (for example, James on good works), while others stress something else. In other words, each book of the Bible has its own special emphasis. With this in mind we shall consider the outlook and purpose of Ecclesiastes.

Throughout the book two important concepts occur over and over. Together they make up the combination which unlocks Solomon's outlook on life.

The first thought is summed up in the terms "meaningless" and "under the sun." Again and again Solomon returns to the initial refrain of Ecclesiastes: "Meaningless! Meaningless! . . . Everything is meaningless" (1:2). This is how he describes life "under the sun," that is, in this world. According to Solomon, life on earth is full of trouble; and even when we find pleasure, it is fleeting and soon disappears like one's breath on a winter day.

This is the first key thought of Ecclesiastes: everything under the sun is, in and of itself, meaningless.

Solomon's repeated use of this concept implies that there is something "beyond the sun." Somewhere out there is something or someone not subject to this meaningless world. That someone, of course, is God. The role of God in our life is the second main thought in Ecclesiastes. Solomon describes God as a stern Judge ("God will bring to judgment both the righteous and the wicked," 3:17), but also as a gracious God who blesses us with countless gifts. The greatest of these gifts is life after death: "The dust returns to the ground it came from, and the spirit returns to God who gave it" (12:7).

When one puts these two main thoughts together, it becomes evident what Solomon has done in Ecclesiastes. He has presented life from two perspectives. First he views the world without God. This view leads to the conclusion, "Everything is meaningless." But he also looks at life with God in control. Here we find many gifts and blessings. We can picture Solomon's twofold presentation thus:

spiritual world
_____
material world

The unbeliever sees nothing beyond the material world, or at best catches an occasional glimpse that there might be something beyond. His sights are focused on what is under the sun. The believer, on the other hand, views life through the eyes of faith.

From his perspective the unbeliever can only conclude that all is meaningless. For him it would be better never to have been born (4:2,3). The believer, however, sees God's hand in everything and so finds peace, contentment and stability in a changing world.

And this brings us from Solomon's outlook to his purpose in writing. He directs us to God and his love for the purpose of strengthening our faith and courage as we carry on "under the sun."

Outline

There are about as many outlines of Ecclesiastes as there are commentators. No two completely agree. Yet amid the disagreement there are two main schools of thought. The first believes that Ecclesiastes can be arranged in some sort of logical outline. The second group argues, with more plausibility, that Ecclesiastes represents a "stream of consciousness" style of writing which defies detailed outlining.

Stream of consciousness, of course, does not necessarily imply disorder. There is a progression of thought through the book. Solomon begins on a note of emptiness. He talks about life without God, "under the sun." But in chapter 7 he changes his emphasis and talks about life under God. He continues to build on this theme (while still weaving in the other) until in the closing verses he declares, "Here is the conclusion of the matter . . . " (12:13).

Alongside this gradual buildup to the conclusion, Solomon, skillful artist that he is, has other things going. His stream of thought is not a steady one, but is distinguished by various ebbs and currents. Just as a stream or river of water has its still spots as well as its rapids, Ecclesiastes alternates between quiet moods and powerful outbursts.

Rather than attempting to make a detailed outline for Ecclesiastes, we'll simply divide the book into these four major sections:

Prologue	(1:1-11)
Life Under the Sun	(1:12-6:12)
Life Under God	(7:1-12:8)
Conclusion	(12:9-14)

Now let's travel along with Solomon and listen to "the words of the Teacher." Although written almost three thousand years ago, they speak directly to our generation. They speak to each of us.

PROLOGUE
ECCLESIASTES 1:1-11

Everything Is Meaningless

1 **The words of the Teacher, son of David, king in Jerusalem:**

This verse actually serves more as a title than as a part of
the book itself. It tells us the name of the book, "The
Teacher" (Greek, "Ecclesiastes"; some commentators retain
the original Hebrew term, "Koheleth"). It tells us that the
Teacher is the "son of David, king in Jerusalem."

With our imagination we can travel back in time to a
faraway age and to a distant city. We are part of an assembly
in ancient Jerusalem, perhaps standing in the courtyard of
the temple.

Before us looms the magnificent temple of Solomon
which took the king's best workmen seven years to build.
Framing the building's doorway are the two massive pillars
with their cast bronze capitals. As a tribute to the Lord, his
God, Solomon had named those pillars Jakin and Boaz,
meaning "he establishes" and "in him is strength."

Suddenly the king and his retinue enter the scene. This is
the great King Solomon who is known throughout the
world for his unmatched wisdom and his fabulous wealth.
He wears a crown of gold and a scarlet robe. But as our
attention moves from the trappings to the man himself, we
see the face of an old man. His eyes betray a weary sorrow.

7

"Meaningless! Meaningless!" says the Teacher,

This is the king whose name would never be forgotten and whose history would live until the end of time. A story of grandeur, yes, but also of tragedy. The sacred historian tells the story, as follows:

As Solomon grew old, his wives turned his heart after other gods, and his heart was not fully devoted to the Lord his God, as the heart of David his father had been. He followed Ashtoreth the goddess of the Sidonians, and Molech the detestable god of the Ammonites. So Solomon did evil in the eyes of the Lord; he did not follow the Lord completely, as David his father had done.

On a hill east of Jerusalem, Solomon built a high place for Chemosh the detestable god of Moab, and for Molech the detestable god of the Ammonites. He did the same for all his foreign wives, who burned incense and offered sacrifices to their gods.

The Lord became angry with Solomon because his heart had turned away from the Lord, the God of Israel, who had appeared to him twice. Although he had forbidden Solomon to follow other gods, Solomon did not keep the Lord's command. So the Lord said to Solomon, "Since this is your attitude and you have not kept my covenant and my decrees, which I commanded you, I will most certainly tear the kingdom away from you and give it to one of your subordinates." (1 Kings 11:4-11)

This is the man who stands before us. His ears must still be ringing with God's judgment. Like the man in Jesus' parable who "would not even look up to heaven, but beat his breast," Solomon must have prayed a thousand times, "God, have mercy on me, a sinner" (Luke 18:13).

We hear no mention of the king's name. Maybe he no longer feels worthy of the name Solomon, which means "Peace." For he had broken peace with God.

This is Solomon the great king . . . and the humbled sinner. He now begins his speech:

> 2"Meaningless! Meaningless!"
> says the Teacher.
> "Utterly meaningless!
> Everything is meaningless."

The first word we hear from the Teacher is anything but encouraging. "Meaningless!" Since this word is so important and occurs so frequently in Ecclesiastes (thirty-seven times), we'll take a minute to look at it. The original idea behind the term is "breath." This idea becomes very vivid on a cold day, when we see our breath, only to see it quickly vanish. St. James captured this thought when he wrote, "What is your life? You are a mist that appears for a little while and then vanishes" (James 4:14). Because it is so fleeting and unstable, life seems to be vain, frustrating, without purpose, empty — in a word, "meaningless."

How accurately this describes life on earth! Beneath all the hustle and bustle, the tinsel and glitter, lurks that terrible sense of emptiness. But it was not that way in Eden, before man fell into sin. It is part of God's judgment upon our sinful world. "The creation was subjected to frustration," declared the Apostle Paul, "not by its own choice, but by the will of the one who subjected it," that is, God himself (Romans 8:20). It is interesting to note that the name Adam and Eve gave their second son, Abel, is the Hebrew word for "meaningless." Perhaps this was their commentary on life after the Fall.

In the remaining verses of his Prologue, Solomon shows how his assertion "Everything is meaningless" does, indeed, describe everything.

10

> ³What does man gain from all his labor
>   at which he toils under the sun?
> ⁴Generations come and generations go,
>   but the earth remains forever.
> ⁵The sun rises and the sun sets,
>   and hurries back to where it rises.
> ⁶The wind blows to the south
>   and turns to the north;
> round and round it goes,
>   ever returning on its course.
> ⁷All streams flow into the sea,
>   yet the sea is never full.
> To the place the streams come from,
>   there they return again.

The king's first example of the meaninglessness of all things hits home convincingly. He speaks of our own human endeavors. When he asks, "What does man gain . . . ?" the implied answer is, "Nothing." In spite of modern technology and machines, work is still hard and discouraging. Ever since the Fall, human labor is under God's curse.

> Cursed is the ground because of you;
>   through painful toil you will eat of it
>   all the days of your life. . . .
> By the sweat of your brow
>   you will eat your food
> until you return to the ground,
>   since from it you were taken;
> for dust you are
>   and to dust you will return. (Genesis 3:17,19)

Each generation grows up, labors, grows old and then returns to the ground. To use Shakespeare's expression, "Life's but a walking shadow, a poor player that struts and frets his hour upon the stage and then is heard no more." This is the "gain" of our labor "under the sun." We have

11

already discussed this phrase, which will recur numerous times in Ecclesiastes. It speaks of our life on earth.

In contrast to the generations which come and go, Solomon states that "the earth remains forever." What irony! In the beginning God created man to rule over all the earth (Genesis 1:26). Yet it is the earth, not man, which remains. Man, created to be the ruler, is swallowed up by earth, the subject. The term "forever" does not mean the earth will *never* come to an end. Although "forever" can refer to eternity, here it signifies a long, indefinite time. Finally God will destroy the present form of this earth and create "a new heaven and a new earth" (Revelation 21:1).

Solomon will return to the futility of all human effort under the sun. But before doing so he demonstrates how nature, too, is caught up in this frustrating condition. He speaks of the sun's rising and setting, only to hurry "back to where it rises." This is not meant to be a scientific statement. It merely reflects our earthbound point of view, in which the sun appears to move across the sky. Even the sun is caught up in the tedium of having to labor day after day after day!

The great novelist Ernest Hemingway went to this verse of Ecclesiastes for the title of one of his books, *The Sun Also Rises*. Like most modern literature, this first novel of Hemingway depicts heroes and heroines who are disillusioned and wearied with life.

Next Solomon talks about the wind. It blows south, then turns north — "round and round it goes." The wind is constantly moving, moving. And for what? It all seems so meaningless.

The ancient world spoke of four elements which made up nature: earth, air, fire and water. In pointing to the earth, wind and sun, Solomon alludes to the first three. Now he turns to the fourth, water. "All the streams flow into the sea. . . . " In this verse the king pictures the water cycle. But, again, he is not attempting to speak in scientific terms. He is only giving another example to show that everything under the sun is meaningless.

We look at nature and see nothing permanent — except the continual change. This restlessness is what St. Paul describes as creation's "groaning" (Romans 8:22). In demonstrating that all of nature is in this condition, Solomon reemphasizes the truth that true satisfaction and rest are not to be found in anything created.

Now the king goes on to show the turmoil within each soul, as it struggles for certainty in this world of flux:

> 8 All things are wearisome,
>   more than one can say.
> The eye never has enough of seeing,
>   or the ear its fill of hearing.
> 9 What has been will be again,
>   what has been done will be done again;
>   there is nothing new under the sun.
> 10 Is there anything of which one can say,
>   "Look! This is something new"?
> It was here already, long ago;
>   it was here before our time.
> 11 There is no remembrance of men of old,
>   and even those who are yet to come
> will not be remembered
>   by those who follow.

"All things are wearisome." According to Solomon, everything is so tiresome that one can't even describe it.

What a contrast this verse makes with St. John's words concerning Jesus: "Jesus did many other things as well. If every one of them were written down, I suppose that even the whole world would not have enough room for the books that would be written"! (John 21:25) This is the exclamation

13

of a man whose soul has found rest in Christ and his promise, "Come to me, all you who are weary and burdened, and I will give you rest" (Matthew 11:28). In Christ everything is new and fresh beyond description.

But Solomon is not talking about that. He is talking about the person who is living without God. This individual is constantly looking and listening, but never satisfied. New styles of dress continually appear, only to be discarded for a different "look." The popular music charts are constantly fluctuating, as people want a new sound. Why? Because the old so quickly becomes wearisome.

The king goes on to show that for all the searching there really is "nothing new under the sun." Just what does Solomon mean by this? Aren't there many things of which it can be said, "Look! This is something new"? No doubt our modern materialistic age would like to take issue with Solomon's words. Look at all the new accomplishments of technology. Aren't spaceships, television, micro-wave ovens and computers new? It seems that Solomon's statement invites contradiction. Yet this is the case only after a superficial reading. Solomon's concern here is not with "things." Nor at this point is he talking about Christ and the gospel. He is relating the human condition: "The eye never has enough of seeing, or the ear its fill of hearing." The desperate state of human restlessness does not change from one generation to the next.

Throughout the Prologue Solomon describes the *fallen* world. It is the bleak picture of a creation under the curse of sin, completely unable to introduce anything "new" for its own salvation.

As we've seen, when the king first began describing this meaningless life, he hit us at a very personal level — the futility of our own efforts ("What does a man gain from all his labor . . . ?"). As he closes his Prologue, Solomon brings our thoughts back to what bothers us the most. It is not the rivers' ceaseless flow into the sea or the wearisome rising and setting of the sun that disturbs most people. Rather, it is this, that *my* labor seems futile and *my* life is going to end and be forgotten.

With the statement, "There is no remembrance of men . . . ," Solomon once again invites contradiction. Certainly people are remembered. But they are not remembered as they should be or as they would like to be. One generation after another commits the same sins of greed and hatred and lust. Although history records many examples of God's judgment upon nations and individuals, we do not remember what happened to others and apply it to ourselves.

And even if the names and deeds of certain individuals might be passed on, this thought affords no comfort. To quote from Shakespeare again, "The evil that men do lives after them. The good is oft interred with their bones."

Ancient civilizations built great monuments to immortalize their outstanding leaders. Who today remembers them as they hoped to be remembered? Who really cares about the ancient Romans or Greeks or Egyptians? Who in future generations will appreciate the accomplishments of our age? Much less, who is going to care about the struggles and achievements that mean so much to you and me?

So we see that future generations are of no help to us. They will be caught up in the unbreakable cycle of this meaningless existence, just as we are.

On this thought the king ends his powerful Prologue.

*"I have seen all things that are done under the sun;
all of them are meaningless, a chasing after the wind."*

16

LIFE UNDER THE SUN
ECCLESIASTES 1:12-6:12

Let's for a moment again picture ourselves back in ancient Jerusalem, listening to Solomon. Now the teacher-king pauses. Our attention moves across the valley and toward the hills around the city of Jerusalem. In the distance we watch a man coax a heavily packed donkey toward the city. He's probably on his way to the market. We think of what Solomon has just said, "What does a man gain from all his labor at which he toils under the sun?" A thousand years from now that scene will still be the same. People coming from the villages into the city. Selling. Buying. New generations will have come and gone " . . . and even those who are yet to come will not be remembered by those who follow."

Our musing is interrupted as the king again begins to speak. We notice a scribe at Solomon's side taking down the king's words.

Instead of talking about the world and people in general, the king now becomes very personal. He talks about himself.

Wisdom Is Meaningless

12I, the Teacher, was king over Israel in Jerusalem. 13I devoted myself to study and to explore by wisdom all that is done under heaven. What a heavy burden God has laid on men! 14I have seen all the things that are done under the sun; all of them are meaningless, a chasing after the wind.

15What is twisted cannot be straightened;
what is lacking cannot be counted.

Without referring to himself by name, Solomon again mentions his prominent position. He isn't boasting, but merely showing that he was in as good a position as anyone to experience life to the fullest. And having lived life to the fullest, Solomon found how empty it could be.

As the king starts recounting his life, he begins with the topic of wisdom. This is only natural, since it was wisdom that had made King Solomon famous throughout the world. The Scriptures record the extent of his wisdom and fame.

> God gave Solomon wisdom and very great insight, and a breadth of understanding as measureless as the sand on the seashore. Solomon's wisdom was greater than the wisdom of all the men of the East, and greater than all the wisdom of Egypt. He was wiser than any other man. . . .

> And his fame spread to all the surrounding nations. He spoke three thousand proverbs and his songs numbered a thousand and five. He described plant life, from the cedar of Lebanon to the hyssop that grows out of walls. He also taught about animals and birds, reptiles and fish. Men of all nations came to listen to Solomon's wisdom, sent by all the kings of the world, who had heard of his wisdom. (1 Kings 4:29-34)

With this vast intellectual treasury, wise King Solomon set out to discover the meaning of life on earth or, as he also calls it, life "under heaven." The first thing he observed was the most obvious: "What a heavy burden God has laid on men!" The expression Solomon uses for "men" literally means "the sons of man," that is, the sons of Adam. Again our thoughts are drawn back to the early history of mankind and to everything it means to be a descendant of the first man and woman. We are conceived and born in sin, as

Solomon's father David declared in Psalm 51. Mankind struggles under the curse of sin. All this is part of the "heavy burden" to which God has subjected fallen creation.

Solomon continues, "I have seen all the things that are done under the sun." We shouldn't get the idea that Solomon was a detached observer of life. No, his seeing life included experiencing it.

He came to know from experience that everything is meaningless and "a chasing after the wind." The old King James Version translates this expression "vexation of spirit." Since the Hebrew word for wind and spirit is the same, either might fit the tone of Ecclesiastes. Yet the idiom "chasing the wind" seems to give us the better picture. In and of themselves, all human endeavors are but futile attempts to grab hold of the wind. You clench it in your fist and what do you have? A handful of nothing! No matter how much you see and learn, that's what you end up with.

Along with Solomon and a few others, the Greek philosopher Socrates (460-399 B.C.) stands as one of history's greatest thinkers. His search for wisdom led to a conclusion not unlike Solomon's: "I know nothing except the fact of my ignorance." Human wisdom cannot find the meaning of life.

King Solomon now inserts a little proverb into his speech: "What is twisted cannot be straightened; what is lacking cannot be counted." He's saying something like, "That's the way it is. You can't change it." You can't count what isn't even there! Likewise it is sheer folly for fallen man to think he can find a way to escape his condition. The resources and wisdom for such an escape lie beyond his grasp. As a matter of fact, he cannot even conceive of what they might be!

16I thought to myself, "Look, I have grown and increased in wisdom more than anyone who has ruled over Jerusalem before me; I have experienced much of wisdom and knowledge."17Then I

applied myself to the understanding of wisdom, and also of madness and folly, but I learned that this, too, is a chasing after the wind.
    **[18]For with much wisdom comes much sorrow;
    the more knowledge, the more grief.**

Was Solomon being too pessimistic in his evaluation of wisdom? As if to assure us, and perhaps himself, he reminds us of his unsurpassed wisdom and knowledge. No one could speak with more authority on the subject than King Solomon.

In comparing himself to all who ruled over Jerusalem, Solomon is not just thinking of his father David. David was the first Israelite king in Jerusalem, but Jerusalem had had other kings before David. Back in Abraham's time Melchizedek was "king of Salem," the old name for Jerusalem (Genesis 14:18). In Joshua's day Jerusalem was ruled by a man named Adoni-Zedek (Joshua 10:1). No doubt there were many others whose names have not come down to us. Yet none of them excelled Solomon in knowledge and wisdom — that is, in knowing facts and in the ability to understand and apply them.

After examining the shortcomings of wisdom, the king turned to "madness and folly." Maybe we can find meaning in life by abandoning wisdom, thought Solomon. This is similar to the modern day despair over finding meaning and value in conventional wisdom. For all the discoveries of science, it hasn't brought man any closer to knowing what life is all about. So people turn from reason to un-reason, rushing headlong into the occult, or drugs, or alcohol, or Eastern mysticism. This, too, is "a chasing after the wind."

With another little proverb set in verse form, Solomon gives this conclusion of his experiments with wisdom: " . . . the more knowledge, the more grief." This is where human wisdom inevitably leads. To gain insight into the world's miserable condition isn't pleasant. And what makes it even sadder is the awareness of one's inability to change things.

There is, however, a wisdom that doesn't lead to grief. Jesus spoke of it when he said, "The Queen of the South . . . came from the ends of the earth to listen to Solomon's wisdom, and now one greater than Solomon is here" (Matthew 12:42). For real, lasting wisdom we must turn to that One who is greater than Solomon. In Christ "are hidden all the treasures of wisdom and knowledge" (Colossians 2:3).

Instead of turning to that godly wisdom (which he had known as a young man) Solomon turned away from it. He directed his search toward pleasure.

Pleasures Are Meaningless

2 **I thought in my heart, "Come now, I will test you with pleasure to find out what is good." But that also proved to be meaningless. ²"Laughter," I said, "is foolish. And what does pleasure accomplish?" ³I tried cheering myself with wine, and embracing folly — my mind still guiding me with wisdom. I wanted to see what was worthwhile for men to do under heaven during the few days of their lives.**

Perhaps we find it strange that Solomon says, "I *thought* in my *heart*." That's only because our concept of heart is much different from the ancient Hebrew's. To us "heart" means either the physical organ or the emotional side of a person. The Jews rarely referred to the heart in a strictly physical sense, but as that which included man's entire inner life of thoughts, will, emotions and personality. The Hebrew word for heart contains a wide range of meanings. It occurs three times in these three verses and each time is translated in a different way: heart (verse 1), myself (verse 3), mind (verse 3).

21

His experiment with wisdom had led to emptiness. And so the king gave himself — his heart — to the pursuit of pleasure. Before he even gets into the details of this pursuit, Solomon presents the results. He found living for pleasure meaningless and foolish; he could only shake his head and wonder, "What does pleasure accomplish?"

Solomon maintains that while he pampered himself with pleasure, his mind was "still guiding [him] with wisdom." He didn't give himself over to mindless debauchery and drunkenness. No, he wanted to have his cake and eat it too, to lick the honey and avoid the gall. Solomon wanted to keep his senses while indulging himself so he could determine what was "worthwhile" to do with one's life.

In spite of Solomon's efforts at self-control, the picture we see is that of a desperate man, groping anywhere he can to find meaning in life. How far King Solomon had drifted from his youth, when in humility he knelt before the Lord and prayed, "Give your servant a discerning heart to govern your people and to distinguish between right and wrong. For who is able to govern this great people of yours?" (1 Kings 3:9) As Solomon describes himself in Ecclesiastes, he had become a man who was trying to get by without God.

Many people never go beyond "cheering themselves with wine, and embracing folly." Drinking and laughter seem to be the be-all and end-all for many. Even when engaged in with restraint, pleasure can become an addiction. It can become a god which controls our lives.

The Lord Jesus may have based one of his parables on these verses of Ecclesiastes. The parable describes a man who said to himself, "You have plenty of good things laid up for many years. Take life easy; eat, drink and be merry" (Luke 12:19). God's verdict on this man was severe: "You fool!" Such is the Creator's judgment of those who live for nothing but eating, drinking and amusement.

King Solomon's pursuit of pleasure did not end with wine and laughter. He goes on to relate how it included the joys of accomplishment and of acquiring possessions.

4I undertook great projects: I built houses for myself and planted vineyards. 5I made gardens and parks and planted all kinds of fruit trees in them. 6I made reservoirs to water groves of flourishing trees. 7I bought male and female slaves and had other slaves who were born in my house. I also owned more herds and flocks than anyone in Jerusalem before me. 8I amassed silver and gold for myself, and the treasure of kings and provinces. I acquired men and women singers, and a harem as well — the delights of the heart of man. 9I became greater by far than anyone in Jerusalem before me. In all this my wisdom stayed with me.

Now the king turns from personal indulgence to personal achievement. In verses 4-6 he describes what he built for himself. Notable by its absence from this list is Solomon's greatest architectural achievement — the temple. But, of course, that would not fit in here. Built for the glory of the eternal God, the temple's purpose far transcended the self-serving projects here described with the constant repetition of "I."

Solomon begins by telling us that he not only built, but also that he carried out his projects in a grandiose way. "I undertook great projects." He then proceeds to enumerate his accomplishments. "I built houses for myself." 1 Kings 7 describes Solomon's palaces.

> It took Solomon thirteen years [compared with seven for the temple], to complete the construction of his palace. . . .
>
> He built the throne hall, the Hall of Justice, where he was to judge, and he covered it with cedar from floor to ceiling. And the palace in which he was to live, set farther back, was similar in design.

Solomon also made a palace like this hall for Pharaoh's daughter, whom he had married. . . . (1 Kings 7:1-12)

"I planted vineyards." The Song of Songs says of this, "Solomon had a vineyard in Baal Hamon; he let out his vineyard to tenants. Each was to bring for its fruit a thousand shekels of silver" (Song of Songs 8:11). Perhaps because the king had vineyards, it became the fashion throughout Israel: "During Solomon's lifetime Judah and Israel, from Dan to Beersheba, lived in safety, each man under his own vine and fig tree" (1 Kings 4:25).

"I made gardens and parks for myself. . . ." The word for parks is *pardes*, possibly of Persian or Eastern origin, and the word from which our term "paradise" comes. In this statement we again see the luxury of Solomon's reign, bringing to mind images of the "hanging gardens" of Babylon or of the gardens of the kings of Persia. It is still a source of pride and a sign of wealth among rich people of the Middle East to have gardens with "all kinds of fruit trees in them."

"I made reservoirs. . . ." Some 500 years after Solomon's time Nehemiah mentioned the "King's Pool" in Jerusalem (Nehemiah 2:14). The Jewish historian Josephus (A.D. 37-95) called this "Solomon's Pool." The function of Solomon's reservoirs was to furnish water for his many trees.

"I bought male and female slaves. . . ." The king has already described his search for pleasures as including partying and projects. Now he introduces a third and final element, also beginning with "p"; his possessions. It seems that here, too, Solomon did not hold back. We are told that when the Queen of Sheba visited Solomon, she was "overwhelmed" (1 Kings 10:5) at "the attending servants in their robes," among other things. With all his servants, the picture is once again that of an oriental potentate of fabulous wealth and power.

"I also owned more herds and flocks. . . . " It is interesting that Solomon proceeds directly from his servants to his cattle and sheep. Had he in his fallen state looked upon his slaves as mere chattel? King Solomon owned more livestock than anyone before him in Jerusalem. This might help explain how at the dedication of the temple he could sacrifice 22,000 cattle and 120,000 sheep and goats! (1 Kings 8:63)

"I amassed silver and gold for myself. . . . " The book of Kings has much to say concerning Solomon's huge treasures.

> The weight of the gold that Solomon received yearly was 666 talents [about 25 tons]. . . .

> All King Solomon's goblets were gold, and all the household articles in the Palace of the Forest of Lebanon were pure gold. Nothing was made of silver, because silver was considered of little value in Solomon's day. . . .

> Year after year, everyone who came brought a gift — articles of silver and gold, robes, weapons and spices, and horses and mules. . . .

> The king made silver as common in Jerusalem as stones. . . . (1 Kings 10)

"I acquired men and women singers, and a harem. . . . " Along with everything else, Solomon saw to it that he could enjoy music and women. The terms translated "harem" is rendered as "musical instruments" in the King James. But the rare Hebrew combination of words quite probably refers to a harem and its delights. This, too, fits the account of 1 Kings: "He had seven hundred wives of royal birth and three hundred concubines" (1 Kings 11:3).

Amid all this splendor and glory, Solomon alleges, "My wisdom stayed with me." Though he had departed from the Lord, the king still had been able to maintain a sense of balance. In his state of apostasy he would not have been

inclined to acknowledge it, but it was only God's grace that
kept Solomon from going the way so many other absolute
rulers have gone, the way of overindulgence to ultimate
ruin.

> [10]I denied myself nothing my eyes desired;
>   I refused my heart no pleasure.
> My heart took delight in all my work,
>   and this was the reward for all my labor.
> [11]Yet when I surveyed all that my hands had done
>   and what I had toiled to achieve,
> everything was meaningless, a chasing after the wind;
>   nothing was gained under the sun.

Verse 10 summarizes Solomon's pursuit of pleasure. He
kept nothing back. "My eyes desired" is literally "my eyes
asked." Like a spoiled child, Solomon got whatever he
wanted.

He talks about delighting in his work. No doubt his delight
lay in the achievement as well as in the work itself. So we see
that Solomon did find some passing enjoyment in life.

Nevertheless, he points out in the next verse that even all
this wealth and pleasure did not really satisfy him. The great
king had everything a man could want and still found it
lacking!

Again Solomon shows how he had fallen from faith. He
had come to call his accomplishments, "the work of *my*
hands" and "the labor at which *I* toiled." Later we'll see how
Solomon attributes earthly blessings to God. But in recounting his experiences here, he takes the viewpoint of natural
man, who sees only his own efforts but fails to see the hidden
God who has given him success.

And to what conclusion does Solomon come? He repeats
the sad refrain, "Everything was meaningless, a chasing
after the wind; nothing was gained under the sun."

How powerfully this section of Ecclesiastes speaks to our generation! Comparisons to decadent Rome are frequent but somewhat out of place. Ours is not yet a society given to unbridled drunkenness and lasciviousness. No, it is pleasure "with wisdom" and restraint that is more our weakness. Fine foods and drinks, eating out, the theater and movies, the world of sports and recreation, accomplishments in business, financial gain — all are pursued without overindulgence, lest one lose his competitive edge.

In concluding this section on Solomon's search for meaning in pleasure, we quote these fitting thoughts from the Lutheran commentator Paul Kretzmann:

> Solomon did what so many people have tried out since his time; instead of accepting the statements of God's Word concerning that which is good and beneficial to them, they determine to try out for themselves what is good and so are obliged to learn through many bitter and painful experiences. Solomon, having the means, took every opportunity for his experiment.[1]

Wisdom and Folly Are Meaningless

> [12]Then I turned my thoughts to consider wisdom,
>   and also madness and folly.
> What more can the king's successor do
>   than what has already been done?
> [13]I saw that wisdom is better than folly,
>   just as light is better than darkness.
> [14]The wise man has eyes in his head,
>   while the fool walks in the darkness;
> but I came to realize
>   that the same fate overtakes them both.
> [15]Then I thought in my heart,
> "The fate of the fool will overtake me also.
> What then do I gain by being wise?"

I said in my heart,
"This too is meaningless."
16For the wise man, like the fool, will not be
long remembered;
in days to come both will be forgotten.
Like the fool, the wise man too must die!

Solomon now turns back to a subject he has already introduced — wisdom. First he struggles to demonstrate the advantage of wisdom over folly. Then he discusses the common end of both wise men and fools.

We might wonder why he should return to the subject of wisdom, since he's already treated it (1:12-18). Nevertheless, wisdom is the constant in Solomon's searchings and testings. We have seen, for example, how his indulgence with wine was tempered with wisdom. Because wisdom underlies all of Solomon's testing of life, it is not surprising that he should frequently return to the topic.

In verse 12 Solomon relates his consideration of wisdom to his position as king. He has just finished describing his great accomplishments; now he asks, "What more can the next king do?" In other words, "If I couldn't find satisfaction in the tremendous projects I completed, what reason is there to suppose the next generation will somehow find the answers?" Some three thousand years have passed since Solomon's time. Yet for all the generations that have come and gone, mankind is no closer to finding the meaning of life.

Notice the parallelism in these verses as Solomon compares the wise man with the fool. The difference is like that between light and darkness! Solomon pictures the wise man walking around with his eyes wide open while the fool stumbles about in the darkness. As we observe life it does seem that some people have their wits about them, while others seem to lurch through life, first this way, then that, then another. Yet this advantage of the wise man is not an especially big one. Solomon has previously discussed the tremendous limitations of wisdom under the sun; he has also pointed out the sadness it brings. Now he speaks of the great equalizer between the wise man and the fool — death.

When he says, "The same fate overtakes them both." Solomon doesn't mean mere chance or blind fate. Nowhere does the Bible teach that. The word might better be translated as "event" (King James), or "happening." Solomon is saying, "What happens to the fool will happen to me."

The king's question, "What then do I gain by being wise?" is rhetorical. The answer is obvious. He gains nothing! "This too is meaningless."

In verse 16 Solomon speaks of being forgotten. He has presented this topic in the Prologue (1:11). As biting as death itself is, the oblivion into which all must pass makes death even more bitter. As time marches on, no one will care about those who died years before. Few will even remember.

Of course, Solomon is still speaking of things under the sun. The believer knows there is a gracious God who never forgets his own. "A righteous man will be remembered forever" (Psalm 112:6).

After skillfully building up to it, Solomon ends this section with the "punch line": "Like the fool, the wise man too must die!" All human pride in wisdom is demolished with this statement. Both wise men and fools end up the same, six feet under.

Toil Is Meaningless

[17]So I hated life, because the work that is done under the sun was grievous to me. All of it is meaningless, a chasing after the wind. [18]I hated all the things I had toiled for under the sun, because I must leave them to the one who comes after me. [19]And who knows

whether he will be a wise man or a fool? Yet he will have control over all the work into which I have poured my effort and skill under the sun. This too is meaningless. ²⁰So my heart began to despair over all my toilsome labor under the sun. ²¹For a man may do his work with wisdom, knowledge and skill, and then he must leave all he owns to someone who has not worked for it. This too is meaningless and a great misfortune. ²²What does a man get for all the toil and anxious striving with which he labors under the sun? ²³All his days his work is pain and grief; even at night his mind does not rest. This too is meaningless.

King Solomon's words "I hated life" bring to mind Christ's statement, "The man who loves his life will lose it, while the man who hates his life in this world will keep it for eternal life" (John 12:25). Solomon describes himself as a weary, embittered worldling. Christ speaks of the man of faith who overcomes this dying, sinful world by clinging to that which is eternal. Yet the two are not so far apart as they might at first appear. The person whose heart is filled with despair and hatred of his earthly life is often ripe for the good news of Christ and his victorious love.

Throughout Ecclesiastes 2 there have been passages which remind one of Jesus' parable about the rich fool, who stored up "things for himself" but was not "rich toward God" (Luke 12:13-21). Verse 18 has the same ring to it as God's words to the rich fool, "Then who will get what you have prepared for yourself?" Solomon's concern about the person who will come after him is not simply a generalized statement of truth. He brings it home to his own life. Perhaps when he wrote this he was having serious doubts about his son Rehoboam. As it turned out, Rehoboam did bring many of Solomon's spectacular achievements to ruin (1 Kings 12).

Nine times in this short section King Solomon uses the terms "meaningless" and "under the sun." Solomon is again emphasizing that without God *all* human effort is meaningless.

And it can only lead to despair. Initially Solomon's achievements brought him some happiness (2:10). But as he gave them more thought, he became agitated and despondent.

As if obsessed with the thought, the Teacher repeats the fact that the wealth of an industrious man often falls into the hands of a good-for-nothing. What is it that makes this such "a great misfortune" (literally, "a great evil")? It is one of those things that make life so unfair. Not only does a person struggle and sweat for a lifetime, but he goes down to the grave without any guarantee that what he leaves behind will be appreciated or used wisely. Solomon's question, "What does a man get for the toil and anxious striving?" fits right in with these thoughts.

To complete the picture, Solomon describes the workingman's daytime efforts and nighttime restlessness. What he describes in verse 23 is not an exaggerated, overly pessimistic view of work, but life as it is actually lived. Though written centuries ago by a Jewish king, it could have been written yesterday by an American businessman.

24A man can do nothing better than to eat and drink and find satisfaction in his work. This too, I see, is from the hand of God, 25for without him, who can eat or find enjoyment? 26To the man who pleases him, God gives wisdom, knowledge and happiness, but to the sinner he gives the task of gathering and storing up wealth to hand it over to the one who pleases God. This too is meaningless, a chasing after the wind.

Having examined wisdom, foolishness, pleasure, achievements and everything else under the sun, Solomon has found it all wanting. But life goes on, and the question forces itself upon us, "How, then, shall we live?" The answer to this question fills the rest of Ecclesiastes. Solomon does not, however, say everything at once. He begins gradually by pointing to God's control. In this way the passage before us presents one of those shifts in the flow of thought in Ecclesiastes.

In this life, says Solomon, the best a person can do is "eat and drink and find satisfaction in his work."

But how can one follow the Teacher's advice and "find satisfaction in his work," when, as Solomon has so powerfully demonstrated, labor is meaningless and a chasing after the wind? The king immediately answers that this is possible only "from the hand of God." God's hand symbolizes his power, and that power is boundless. As Jesus said, "With God all things are possible" (Matthew 19:26).

Here faith enters the picture. Only faith in Christ can pierce through this fallen world's dark cloud of vanity to see the bright love and mercy of the almighty God. The person who "pleases God" is none other than the believer. Scripture states, "Without faith it is impossible to please God" (Hebrews 11:6).

Solomon puts the one who pleases God in contrast to "the sinner." Though all are sinners, the term here (verse 26) applies only to the unbelieving, unrepentant sinner. This sinner possesses nothing, while the believer receives all good things.

At first glance this assertion of Solomon doesn't seem to fit with reality. Often the ungodly are very wealthy. With his characteristic ability to see to the heart of the matter, Martin Luther quickly solves the apparent problem: "In short, the pious truly possess the whole world, because they enjoy it with happiness and tranquillity. But the impious do not possess it even when they have it. This is the vanity which the impious possess."[2]

So there is a time and place for labor and its enjoyment. Indeed, there is a time for everything.

32

A Time for Everything

3 There is a time for everything,
and a season for every activity under heaven:
²a time to be born and a time to die,
a time to plant and a time to uproot,
³a time to kill and a time to heal,
a time to tear down and a time to build,
⁴a time to weep and a time to laugh,
a time to mourn and a time to dance,
⁵a time to scatter stones and a time to gather them,
a time to embrace and a time to refrain,
⁶a time to search and a time to give up,
a time to keep and a time to throw away,
⁷a time to tear and a time to mend,
a time to be silent and a time to speak,
⁸a time to love and a time to hate,
a time for war and a time for peace.

These verses form one of the most famous portions of Ecclesiastes. With one short poetic line after another Solomon drives home the truth stated in the first verse: "There is a time for everything."

Verses 2-8 consist of fourteen pairs of opposite words ("be born . . . die." etc.). The use of seven or multiples thereof is common in the Old Testament. We encounter it elsewhere in Ecclesiastes and the Song of Songs. Seven signifies completeness. Here Solomon uses it to include every human activity.

Each word-pair seems to reflect the thought of the neighboring pair within the same verse. For example, in verse 4 "weep . . . laugh" parallels "mourn . . . dance." Or verse 8, "love . . . hate" and "war . . . peace."

Although most of Solomon's thoughts here are self-explanatory, a few comments are in order.

The references to uprooting, healing and building in verses 2 and 3 are seen by some as allusions to God's dealings with his chosen people. Psalm 80:8,9, for instance, states, "You brought a vine out of Egypt; you drove out the nations and planted it. You cleared the ground for it, and it took root and filled the land." Perhaps building on Solomon's words, the Prophet Jeremiah uses similar language with reference to God's people: "I will build them up and not tear down; I will plant them and not uproot them" (Jeremiah 24:6). But even if Solomon is thinking of specific Israelite history, he is also speaking of general human experiences. This is his tendency throughout Ecclesiastes.

Certain commentators see verse 5 as having sexual significance. Jewish scholars took the term "scatter stones" as referring to sexual relations and "gather" as referring to abstinence. In view of the parallelism in the second part of the verse — "a time to embrace . . . refrain" — this suggestion is not without merit.

There is another way to understand this. When Jesus spoke of the destruction of the temple, he described this casting down of stones: "Not one stone will be left on another; every one will be thrown down" (Mark 13:2). If we understand the verse before us in this manner, Solomon is describing the time for building (prosperity) versus the time for destruction. The second half of the verse would fit in an indirect way: the time for embracing is the time of prosperity and the time for refraining is a time of need.

Citing another verse in this section, "to tear" in verse 7 brings to mind the Hebrew practice of tearing a garment in time of anger or sorrow. For example, when Jesus was on trial "the high priest tore his clothes" in anger (Matthew 26:65). In contrast to tear is "mend."

Even hatred and war have their time along with love and peace. Christians are to hate the emptiness of this world; they are also to hate evil (Proverbs 8:13). We are constantly at war with "the powers of this dark world and against the spiritual forces of evil" (Ephesians 6:12); and, if called upon, we should serve our country in time of war. Moreover, God himself exhibits both hatred (Psalm 5:5) and love (John 3:16) for this sinful world.

In any case, we need not insist on this or that picture in these verses. King Solomon is speaking of a time for everything. The examples he gives are general enough to include just that — everything.

The main question in this section of Ecclesiastes is not related to specific details. Rather, it has to do with the thrust of the entire passage. What is Solomon trying to teach us when he says there is a time for everything? Commentators have offered several answers.

Some contend that Solomon here teaches "it is wisdom to do the right thing at the right time."[3] The idea is to know when to do this and when to do that. With the right timing a person will make the most of his opportunities and lead a successful life. As appealing as such an interpretation might be (especially in our humanistic age), it simply does not square with the text. The time of our birth is beyond our control. Likewise the events bringing joy or sorrow into our lives are not in our hands.

Others conclude from these verses that "all the events of life are part of a fixed scheme; they happen to the human being, whether he wills them or not; therefore individual effort is abortive."[4] But Solomon does not intend to squelch human effort. The later chapters of Ecclesiastes are filled with advice on how to live.

The best explanation is that the Teacher here points to God's control. Solomon is showing that everything is in God's hands. God is, in the words of one commentator, "the Governor of this world and the Former of history, who makes even that which is evil subservient to his plan."[5] Rather then aborting human effort, this truth encourages us to follow God's will as revealed in the Scriptures. As God's children we do what we can. Then we leave the outcome in his almighty hands.

⁹What does the worker gain from his toil? ¹⁰I have seen the burden God has laid on men. ¹¹He has made everything beautiful in its time. He has also set eternity in the hearts of men; yet they cannot fathom what God has done from beginning to end. ¹²I know that there is nothing better for men than to be happy and do good while they live. ¹³That every man may eat and drink, and find satisfaction in all his toil — this is the gift of God. ¹⁴I know that everything God does will endure forever; nothing can be added to it and nothing taken from it. God does it, so men will revere him.

> **¹⁵Whatever is has already been,**
> **and what will be has been before;**
> **and God will call the past to account.**

God controls everything. In his infinite wisdom and power he fits everything into his eternal plan, and so "everything is beautiful in its time." The Apostle Paul wrote, "And we know that in all things God works for the good of those who love him, who have been called according to his purpose" (Romans 8:28). To see life's hardships and joys alike as part of this grand scheme, is like viewing life as a beautiful mosaic from the hands of the master Artist.

With this in mind, Solomon returns to the question, "What does the worker gain from his toil?" Why bother to do anything if God is going to do as he pleases anyway? The king offers several answers.

The first lies in the magnificent statement, "He has also set eternity in the hearts of men." Deep within each of us God has placed a longing for that which lasts forever, a longing which life's fleeting experiences are unable to satisfy. Coupled with this longing is an awareness in each of us that this life is not the end. In spite of the apparent futility of human endeavor, man senses that what he does has lasting repercussions. Yet without the gospel of Christ man has no way of knowing how to reach God and eternal life. And the longing for eternity becomes nothing but another irritation and frustration under the sun.

It is interesting that the Hebrew word for eternity basically means "the hidden time." Although we have a natural sense of eternity, we lack a corresponding ability to see into the distant past or future. It is hidden from us. Happily, God has given us some information in the Bible. He tells us something about the beginning and creation (Genesis 1) and about the end — judgment, heaven and hell (the book of Revelation and many other portions of Scripture). He also tells us the way to heaven: through Jesus Christ who is "the way" (John 14:6).

Besides a built-in sense of eternity which gives meaning to our labor, Solomon points to another reason for working. It brings satisfaction. In this life "there is nothing better" than to work and "do good" and enjoy whatever fruits may result from our efforts. Like everything else that's good in life, this ability to find some satisfaction in our labor is "the gift of God."

Every good gift is from God. And what an awesome God he is! Everything he does "will endure forever." No one can take away what God decides to give. If he gives us the greatest gift of all, his love and forgiveness in Christ, then "who shall separate us from the love of Christ?" (Romans 8:35) The answer of course is: nobody shall.

It is foolish to try to add to God's great plans. For example, there is nothing any man can add to God's plan of salvation. Good works add nothing to what Christ has won for mankind. "It is the gift of God — not by works, so that no one can boast" (Ephesians 2:8,9).

It is also foolish and wicked to add to or take away from God's Word. "If anyone adds anything to them [God's words], God will add to him the plagues described in this book. And if anyone takes words away . . . God will take away from him his share in the tree of life and in the holy city [heaven]" (Revelation 22:18,19).

Instead of attempting to add to or subtract from what God says and does, we are simply to worship and revere him.

God's love "endures forever" (Psalm 136). His Word "stands forever" (Isaiah 40:8). Jesus Christ "is the same yesterday and today and forever" (Hebrews 13:8). Thus, "whatever is has already been, and what will be has been before." God's plan of salvation was worked out already before the creation of the world.

The final line of this section can be understood in either of two ways: "God calls back the past" or "God will call the past to account." The first possibility fits with everything Solomon has said up to this point in the chapter. At the proper time God will bring back what is necessary in keeping with his designs. The other understanding of the verse fits with what is about to follow. There the king speaks about God's judgment, a time for calling the past to account.

> ¹⁶And I saw something else under the sun:
>   In the place of judgment—wickedness was there,
>   in the place of justice—wickedness was there.
> ¹⁷I thought in my heart,
>   "God will bring to judgment
>   both the righteous and the wicked,
>   for there will be a time for every activity,
>   a time for every deed."

Often it seems that good, honest labor doesn't pay. Under the sun the opposite frequently appears to be the case. Sin has such a grip on mankind, and the world so teems with wickedness, that evildoers get away with an awful lot. Even where we would expect to find justice, there is none. In Solomon's day, as in ours, courts of justice weren't everything they should have been. When one looks at this it's easy to become cynical like the famous lawyer Clarence Darrow who remarked, "There is no such thing as justice — in or out of court." At times one might even get the notion that crime does pay.

Or does it? The Teacher immediately states that there will come a time of reckoning. "God will bring to judgment both the righteous and the wicked." Then "every deed" will be brought to light.

Along with the sense of eternity, God has placed into people a conscience and a sense of right and wrong (Romans 2:14,15). Nature also testifies that there is a God (Psalm 19:1). Man's natural awareness of his accountability before God helps explain why the world is not completely overrun with wickedness. Yet even man's most righteous activities are not enough to earn salvation. That must come as a gift from God.

18I also thought, "As for men, God tests them so that they may see that they are like the animals. 19Man's fate is like that of the animals; the same fate awaits them both: As one dies, so dies the other. All have the same breath; man has no advantage over the animal. Everything is meaningless. 20All go to the same place; all come from dust, and to dust all return. 21Who knows if the spirit of man rises upward and if the spirit of the animal goes down into the earth?"

22So I saw that there is nothing better for a man than to enjoy his work, because that is his lot. For who can bring him to see what will happen after him?

Earlier Solomon had compared the wise man with the fool. Now he compares all people to animals! In doing this, he again drives home his point: "Everything is meaningless." Under the curse of sin both man and beast must return to dust. In this respect, despite all his achievements "man has no advantage over the animal."

Why does God so "test" man? It's as if God is rubbing mankind's collective face in the dirt and saying, "This is how you measure up." God had created man to rule over all the animals (Genesis 1:26). Now they share the same end in this world: death. This is another strong preachment of God's judgment upon the world.

A footnote in the New International Version indicates that verse 21 may be translated in another way: "Who knows the spirit of man, which rises upward, or the spirit of the animal, which goes down into the earth?" This is quite different from the other rendering. One asks, "Who knows the spirit of man?" The other, "Who knows where the spirit of man goes?" Yet both of these acceptable translations point out the same truth. By himself man is unable to know anything spiritual. He can't know anything about his spiritual life. Nor can he know anything about the spirit's life after death. He is as ignorant in these matters as are the animals.

Left to himself man is likely to conclude he is nothing but a highly evolved animal. Only by a God-given revelation can we learn the truth.

Later Solomon will talk about what awaits man's spirit (12:7). For now, the Teacher simply urges us to enjoy our work. Accept the lot God has given you in life. As to the future, leave that to God.

Oppression, Toil, Friendlessness

4 Again I looked and saw all the oppression that was taking place under the sun:

> I saw the tears of the oppressed —
> and they have no comforter;

power was on the side of their oppressors —
and they have no comforter.
[2]And I declared that the dead,
who had already died,
are happier than the living,
who are still alive.
[3]But better than both
is he who has not yet been,
who has not seen the evil
that is done under the sun.

Once again King Solomon invites us to look with him into the world's misery. Previously he had talked about the world in general and about his own dissatisfaction. Now he focuses on the problems of others, beginning with the oppressed. One commentator, Ernest Hengstenberg, explains the purpose of the Teacher's constant emphasis on human misery: "By thoroughly disgusting us with the world, and by making us realize its absolute vanity, God means to draw us to himself. . . . Through much tribulation must our hold on earthly things be loosened and ourselves enter into the kingdom of God."[6]

Some argue that Solomon could not have authored this section of Ecclesiastes, because his was a peaceful reign, free from the kind of oppression described here. But Solomon did not shut his eyes to what goes on in the world. He is merely observing the normal state of affairs.

Job also observed such unjust oppression and wondered aloud why God seems to do nothing about it. "The groans of the dying rise from the city, and the souls of the wounded cry out for help. But God charges no one with wrongdoing" (Job 23:12). Of course, God does keep account of wrongdoing, even though from our vantage point we can not see the end of his justice.

Nor do we have to look very hard to see oppression in our day. Tyranny abounds throughout the world, and our own land has its share of injustice and lack of concern for the needy. The rich get richer and the poor poorer.

Looking at all this wretchedness, King Solomon decided that it would be better to be dead, or never to have been born in the first place! This is the way it is "under the sun." If all we had were the misery of this world, we might well conclude with the French philosopher Voltaire (1694-1778), "I wish I had never been born." Or, as the British statesman Benjamin Disraeli (1804-1881) observed, "Youth is a blunder; manhood, a struggle; old age, a regret." Eastern religions such as Hinduism and Buddhism have come to similar conclusions; the highest good is to attain nirvana, a state of nothingness. These are the observations of people from all ages and from around the world.

Christians also long to escape this life. With the Apostle Paul we exclaim, "I desire to depart and to be with Christ, which is better by far" (Philippians 1:23). But we also have a purpose for staying here, "I know that I will remain, and I will continue with all of you for your progress and joy in the faith" (Philippians 1:25). Unlike the unbeliever, we have a wonderful place to go when we leave this vale of tears. And unlike him we have something worth sharing while we live on earth — the love of Christ.

⁴And I saw that all labor and all achievement spring from man's envy of his neighbor. This too is meaningless, a chasing after the wind.

> **⁵The fool folds his hands**
> **and ruins himself.**
> **⁶Better one handful with tranquillity**
> **than two handfuls with toil**
> **and chasing after the wind.**

From the topic of oppression, the Teacher returns to that of labor. He presents two wrong attitudes toward work. Both of them are common.

The first we know as "keeping up with the Joneses." Think of it. What motivates people to be successful? Everyone wants to prove himself. How many rags-to-riches stories don't result from people's dreams of someday living on the other side of the tracks and in the right neighborhood? Someone has remarked that people will work harder for luxuries than for life's basic necessities. Many a businessman trying to get ahead puts in longer hours than the individual who is barely scratching out a living. In church work, too, envy can be the hidden motivation for much activity. People want to outshine each other in every area of life.

When the Teacher declares that "all labor and all achievement spring from man's envy," he is speaking about the kind of work which is unable to satisfy. He is referring to the ceaseless activity and striving which in the end are meaningless. In a word, Solomon is describing work done without God.

Often the successful person is contemptuous of those who don't achieve much. Verse 5 appears to be a proverb which Solomon places into the mouth of the hard worker: "The fool folds his hands and ruins himself." True, if a person sits back with his hands folded over his stomach and never uses them constructively, he's going to ruin himself. (The expression "ruins himself" literally means, "he eats his own flesh"!)

Verse 6 seems to be the "fool's" reply. "At least I've got some tranquillity. Look at all your efforts to get ahead. For what? You're just chasing after the wind."

So on the one hand, Solomon points to the person who is driven by envy and has no rest in his attempts to get ahead in the world. On the other hand, he points to the lazy person who has no cares, but lets life slip by without ever using his God-given abilities. Two more examples of life under the sun.

[7] Again I saw something meaningless under the sun:
    [8] There was a man all alone;
        he had neither son nor brother.
    There was no end to his toil,
        yet his eyes were not content with his wealth.
    "For whom am I toiling," he asked,
        "and why am I depriving myself of enjoyment?"
    This too is meaningless —
        a miserable business!
    [9] Two are better than one,
        because they have a good return for their work:
    [10] If one falls down,
        his friend can help him up.
    But pity the man who falls
        and has no one to help him up!
    [11] Also, if two lie down together, they will keep warm.
    But how can one keep warm alone?
    [12] Though one may be overpowered,
        two can defend themselves.
    A cord of three strands is not quickly broken.

The Teacher continues to enumerate life's problems. From the themes of oppression and toil, he takes us to loneliness. Like the labor rooted in envy, this topic hits close to home for many twentieth century Americans. Over half the adult population in this country is single. We hear much talk about alienation and loneliness, among the married as well as the single. It's not that there aren't plenty of people around. But real, lasting friendship is hard to come by in our age of mobility, competition and superficiality.

  It doesn't take long to think of modern day examples to fit Solomon's description of the wealthy, yet lonely, man.

Sometimes very rich and famous people spend their last years living almost like hermits. Names like Howard Hughes and Elvis Presley come to mind.

In verse 8 the words "he asked" are not in the original Hebrew. Nor are there any quotation marks; the ancient Hebrew has no such thing. The translators have supplied these items to clarify that the rich man is speaking to himself. We can see from this interesting little sidelight how thoroughly Solomon put himself into the other man's situation. The Teacher quite simply and naturally slips into the words and thoughts of another. This is the same thing Solomon did earlier in the chapter with the brief exchange between the hard working man and "the fool."

In verses 9-12 Solomon lists four advantages of companionship over friendlessness: Cooperation — "they have a good return for their work." Help in time of need — "if one falls down, his friend can help him up." Warmth — "if two lie together, they will keep warm." (We could extend this warmth to include emotional support and encouragement.) Defense — "two can defend themselves."

And, the king goes on to say, three are even better than two! In many areas of life strength does lie in numbers. The individual Christian who thinks he can get along without a church ("I can read the Bible at home") should keep this in mind. We need the cooperation, help, warmth and defense of those who share the common treasure of faith.

Advancement Is Meaningless

13Better a poor but wise youth than an old but foolish king who no longer knows how to take warning. 14The youth may have come from prison to the kingship, or he may have been born in poverty within his kingdom. 15I saw that all who lived and walked under the sun followed the youth, the king's successor. 16There was no end to all the people who were before them. But those who

came later were not pleased with the successor. This too is meaningless, a chasing after the wind.

It must have been difficult for King Solomon to talk about "an old but foolish king." His own sad example could not have been far from his thoughts or those of his pious contemporaries. Among the ancients age was usually equated with wisdom. For an old person to be foolish, then, was a disgrace.

Solomon proceeds to tell of a wise youth who "may have come from prison to the kingship, or he may have been born in poverty. . . . " Since the youth's background is not specific, we may conclude that Solomon is not talking about a particular individual. He is telling a story which often repeats itself with slight variations in the details. No doubt Solomon himself "saw" it happen more than once in the many kingdoms of his day.

The young man arises from humble beginnings, overcomes obstacles, becomes king in place of the foolish old ruler, and enjoys immense popularity. "All who lived and walked under the sun followed the youth. . . . There was no end to all the people before him."

Once the wise youth is settled in power, some of his glory begins to tarnish. Like any other mortal, he makes mistakes. Perhaps he ends up as "an old but foolish king who no longer knows how to take warning." And "those who came later" — both people and rulers — "were not pleased" with him.

The cycle is then complete, awaiting only another young man who would rise from obscurity and take over the throne.

History is full of people who fit this general pattern. The Bible relates how Joseph went from prison to the second highest position in Egypt (Genesis 41). Despite his rise to power, Joseph kept his wisdom and faith. Most stories don't end so happily. Israel's first king, Saul, started in humility. But after he came to power he fell from faith and eventually ended his own life (1 Samuel 31). David and Solomon began their reigns well, but both fell into grievous sins while king. David also had to contend with the rebellion of his son Absalom, who tried to seize the throne (2 Samuel 15-18). The reign of the Roman Emperor Nero started out with hope and rejoicing but became notorious for its depravity and cruelty. Many modern day presidents have known both the heights of popularity and the depths of public derision.

What holds true in the world of rulers and politicians also applies to the fields of business, sports and entertainment. Many people rise only to fall. Others begin well only to become corrupt and incompetent. Today's hero easily becomes tomorrow's has-been.

"This too is meaningless, a chasing after the wind."

Stand in Awe of God

5 **Guard your steps when you go to the house of God. Go near to listen rather than to offer the sacrifice of fools, who do not know that they do wrong.**
> **²Do not be quick with your mouth,**
>   **do not be hasty in your heart**
>   **to utter anything before God.**
> **God is in heaven**
>   **and you are on earth,**
>   **so let your words be few.**
> **³As a dream comes when there are many cares,**
>   **so the speech of a fool when there are many words.**

This section marks another important turning point in the Teacher's stream of thought. He has said much about the meaningless life under the sun, without God. He has also shown that God is in control and, whether we realize it or not, we are completely dependent on him (chapter 3). Now King Solomon brings God into the picture even more. He talks about our duty to worship God. At this point Solomon also begins to involve the reader or listener more directly. Instead of talking about the world or himself or others, he uses the second person pronoun: "you."

Solomon leads us "to the house of *God*." Perhaps you've noticed that when Solomon speaks about God he avoids using the common term "the Lord." Throughout Ecclesiastes he *never* uses that title but speaks only of "God." "Yahweh," or "the Lord" was the special name God revealed to his Old Testament nation Israel. It represented God's qualities of free and steadfast grace (Exodus 34:4-7). The promises of forgiveness and the coming Savior were closely linked to the name "the Lord," which occurs over 5,000 times in the Old Testament. Possibly because he's speaking in general terms for all nations, King Solomon only uses the more general word for God. Or, as others have suggested, it might be as a sign of "his unworthiness of the privileges of a son of the Covenant that he avoids the name of the Lord of the Covenant."[7]

In Solomon's day "the house of God" was the magnificent temple the king had built in Jerusalem. This was the center of worship for God's people. The annual festivals saw Jerusalem packed with pilgrims who had come up to the temple. The great altar of sacrifice in front of the temple daily filled the air with smoke from the endless burnt offerings.

Solomon warns all going to the house of God, "Guard your steps." That is, "Be careful." The teacher-king immediately adds the reason for this care, "Go near to listen rather than to offer the sacrifice of fools." This is similar to the words the Prophet Samuel had spoken to King Saul, "Does the Lord delight in burnt offerings and sacrifices as much as in obeying the voice of the Lord? To obey is better than sacrifice, and to heed is better than the fat of rams" (1 Samuel 15:22). Saul had not obeyed God's command to completely destroy his enemies the Amalekites and all their possessions. He had kept some back. When Samuel confronted him with this, Saul protested, "The soldiers took sheep and cattle from the plunder, the best of what was devoted to God, in order to sacrifice them to the Lord your God" (1 Samuel 15:21). Saul had thought he could get around God's command by offering him some sacrifices. The result was tragic. "Because you have rejected the word of the Lord," Samuel pronounced, "he has rejected you as king" (1 Samuel 15:23).

This is a warning to people today who think they can fool God in similar ways. They might feel they can disregard his stern decrees about cheating, cursing, drunkenness or divorce. To appease God they become active members at church and contribute generously of money and time. This is "the sacrifice of fools."

Of first importance is hearing and taking to heart the Word which is read and proclaimed in church. Jesus said, "Blessed . . . are those who hear the word of God and obey it" (Luke 11:28). The fool, however, blindly thinks he's doing all right by going through the motions. To the Hebrews a fool was not someone lacking intelligence, but a person lacking in morals and a right relationship with God.

Solomon goes on to state that while we should be eager to listen to God's word, we should not speak too hastily. James put it this way, "Everyone should be quick to listen, slow to speak. . . . " (James 1:19). Just as we have a natural sinful inclination to try to buy God off, we also have the tendency to make rash promises. Often in an hour of need people promise to do all sorts of great things, if God will get them out of their difficulty. Then, once the trouble has passed, the promise is forgotten.

The tendency to say too much is a mark of the fool. Solomon says that many words come from a fool, just as dreams often accompany a troubled mind. With this remark he is simply making a comparison: empty words flow from a fool's mouth as dreams flutter through a restless mind.

Jesus also tells us to avoid wordiness when speaking to God. "When you pray, do not keep on babbling like pagans, for they think they will be heard because of their many words. Do not be like them, for your Father knows what you need before you ask him" (Matthew 6:7,8). We earthbound creatures need to remember we are dealing with our almighty Father in heaven. We can be honest with him. We can't fool him with a lot of empty words.

4When you make a vow to God, do not delay in fulfilling it. He has no pleasure in fools; fulfill your vow. 5It is better not to vow than to make a vow and not fulfill it. 6Do not let your mouth lead you into sin. And do not protest to the⌊ temple ⌋ messenger, "My vow was a mistake." Why should God be angry at what you say and destroy the work of your hands? 7Much dreaming and many words are meaningless. Therefore stand in awe of God.

Still speaking of our relationship to God, Solomon urges us to follow through on our vows to God. The first vow recorded in Scripture was made by Jacob. When he left home as a young man, he promised, "If God will be with me and will watch over me on this journey . . . then the Lord will be my God . . . and of all that you [God] give me I will give you back a tenth" (Genesis 28:20-22). Years later Jacob returned to Bethel, the place he made that vow. He built an altar there and, we can assume, in thankfulness fulfilled his promise (Genesis 35:7). On another occasion, Hannah vowed that if God gave her a son she would "give him to the Lord for all the days of his life" (1 Samuel 1:11). She did have a son and gave him to God's work after naming him

Samuel, which means "God hears." God had heard her prayer and blessed her with a son.

Vows played an important role in the life of many Old Testament people. God even laid down specific rules for vows (Deuteronomy 23:21-23), which Solomon's words echo closely. These vows were not to be taken lightly or dismissed with a shrug of the shoulders. "Do not protest to the temple messenger, 'My vow was a mistake.' " The "temple messenger" might refer to the priest. Since "messenger" and "angel" are the same word in Hebrew, the King James Bible translates it as angel. Possibly it refers to the Angel of the Lord, that is, Christ himself. Regardless who the messenger is, God takes note of the vow.

But what if a vow really is a mistake? A person might, for instance, wrongly vow to get even with someone who's hurt him. Such vows need to be dismissed in the light of God's Word, which forbids a vengeful spirit and teaches us to love our enemies. Solomon is rather speaking of those God-pleasing promises we make.

For the Old Testament people vows were optional. It's the same today. We don't have to make promises. But if we do, we should be serious. Baptismal sponsors promise to remember the child in their prayers. At their Confirmation young men and women vow "to remain true to the triune God, even unto death." Some Christians pledge to offer a definite amount of money to the Lord in keeping with their income. People who get married vow to remain faithful "till death."

These are all vows before God. They are not just so many empty words to be forgotten like last night's dream. We are to "stand in awe of God." The Lord Jesus warns that God will call people to account for their "careless" speech (Matthew 12:36,37). Let us take this to heart.

51

Riches Are Meaningless

[8]If you see the poor oppressed in a district, and justice and rights denied, do not be surprised at such things; for one official is eyed by a higher one, and over them both are others higher still. [9]The increase from the land is taken by all; the king himself profits from the fields.

[10]Whoever loves money never has money enough;
    whoever loves wealth is never satisfied with his income.
    This too is meaningless.
[11]As goods increase,
    so do those who consume them.
And what benefit are they to the owner
    except to feast his eyes on them?
[12]The sleep of a laborer is sweet,
    whether he eats little or much,
but the abundance of a rich man
    permits him no sleep.

Solomon has just spoken of sublime things, our relation to God in heaven. Now he is down to earth again and talking about a very earthly subject. Once more he demonstrates how meaningless riches are.

King Solomon's father David had written in the Psalm, "The earth is the Lord's, and everything in it" (Psalm 24:1). Because of his love, God gives the earth for man's use. "He makes grass grow for the cattle, and plants for man to cultivate — bringing forth food from the earth" (Psalm 104:14). But instead of cultivating the earth with thanksgiving and sharing its crops in love, sinful man has seen the land as a means for selfish ends. A poor man works the land. Someone over him collects taxes, while another higher official makes sure that he also gets a cut of it. And so on up the line. "The increase from the land is taken by all; the king himself profits from the fields."

Behind this greed lies an insatiable lust for money. Those who love money never have enough. The elder Rockefeller was once asked, "How much money does it take to satisfy a person?" The billionaire snapped back, "Always a little more!"

Besides not being able to satisfy, riches bring other problems. The more one acquires, the more hangers-on there are to consume the goods. Or a man might become so wealthy that he has more riches than he could ever use; all he can do is "feast his eyes on them." For all his wealth, such a man isn't much better off than a poor man who also feasts his eyes on riches he can't make use of. Still another person might have enough money to be a man of leisure, but for one reason or another is never able to enjoy his leisure.

In contrast to the greedy man, the Teacher portrays the godly laborer whose sleep "is sweet." Although spoiled by the fall into sin, work is still a blessing. It's what the Lord expects of all his able-bodied people. "If a man will not work, he shall not eat" (1 Thessalonians 3:10). If work is available, do it.

13I have seen a grievous evil under the sun:
>   wealth hoarded to the harm of its owner,
14   or wealth lost through some misfortune,
>   so that when he has a son
>   there is nothing left for him.
15Naked a man comes from his mother's womb,
>   and as he comes, so he departs.
>   He takes nothing from his labor
>   that he can carry in his hand.
16This too is a grievous evil:
>   As a man comes, so he departs,
>   and what does he gain,
>   since he toils for the wind?
17All his days he eats in darkness,
>   with great frustration, affliction and anger.

Not only can striving for riches bring no satisfaction, but once a person has them they bring all kinds of new concerns. In his greed a man might hoard his wealth. He becomes so obsessed with it that he becomes a slave to it. There is no guarantee that he won't lose it through some calamity anyway. We shouldn't get the idea from the word translated "misfortune" that Solomon is talking about bad luck. As was mentioned earlier, the Bible rules out the concepts of fate or luck or chance. God is always working behind the scenes. He is in control.

Even if a man should become rich and maintain his wealth for a lifetime, there soon comes a time when he has to leave it behind. It's said that when Alexander the Great lay on his deathbed he commanded that contrary to the usual custom his hands not be wrapped. He wanted everyone to see his empty hands as he was carried to his grave. And so in death the great conqueror and king of nations was on equal terms with the poorest beggar.

When Job lost all his wealth, he said, "Naked I came from my mother's womb, and naked I will depart. The Lord gave and the Lord has taken away; may the name of the Lord be praised" (Job 1:21). Solomon is probably thinking of Job's words. (Some feel that Solomon wrote the book of Job, in which case he would have been intimately familiar with Job's words.) Notice that in the Ecclesiastes passages Solomon does not add Job's words of trust in the Lord. The man living under the sun without God has no such comfort.

St. Paul probably had both Job and Ecclesiastes in mind when he wrote,

> Godliness with contentment is great gain. For we brought nothing into the world, and we can take nothing out of it. But if we have food and clothing, we will be content with that. People who want to get rich fall into temptation and a trap and

into many foolish and harmful desires that plunge men into ruin and destruction. For the love of money is a root of all kinds of evil. Some people, eager for money, have wandered from the faith and pierced themselves with many griefs. (1 Timothy 6:6-10)

Solomon's words about eating in darkness might depict the greedy man working late into the night before taking time to eat. More likely, they portray the sadness which so often accompanies riches. "Frustration, affliction and anger" — that's what people get if riches are their obsession. And in the end they inherit not even the wind which blows across their grave.

Greed has led to the downfall of many a man. It was also one reason God destroyed Sodom. "Now this was the sin of your sister Sodom: she and her daughters were arrogant, overfed and unconcerned; they did not help the poor and needy. . . . Therefore I did away with them" (Ezekiel 16:49,50). God makes it clear that Sodom's sinful lusts were not just sexual; they included greed and selfishness. Solomon's warning against greed certainly applies also to our generation.

[18]Then I realized that it is good and proper for a man to eat and drink, and to find satisfaction in his toilsome labor under the sun during the few days of life God has given him — for this is his lot. [19]Moreover, when God gives any man wealth and possessions, and enables him to enjoy them, to accept his lot and be happy in his work — this is a gift of God. [20]He seldom reflects on the days of his life, because God keeps him occupied with gladness of heart.

Here Solomon paints a much happier scene than in the previous verses. He shows us a household where godliness and contentment reign in place of greed and discontent. He portrays a child of God, a believer.

55

Although labor remains "toilsome" for this person, he is able "to find satisfaction" in it. God enables him to enjoy his possessions and to "be happy in his work." This worker accepts his lot in life — his talents, opportunities and possessions. His work is not a frenzied attempt to pile up riches. He works because it's the lot God has given him in life. In the words of St. Paul, we are to do "all for the glory of God" (1 Corinthians 10:31). We try to make the best possible use of our life as a way of saying thanks to God for the gift of life and for his many other blessings.

Finally, the godly man "seldom reflects . . . because God keeps him occupied with gladness of heart." He isn't filled with worry but with gladness. Jesus says, "Do not worry about your life, what you will eat or drink; or about your body, what you will wear. Is not life more important than food, and the body more important than clothes? . . . But seek first [God's] kingdom and his righteousness, and all these things will be given to you as well" (Matthew 6:25-34).

Where does one find gladness of heart and the kingdom of God and his righteousness? They come only from listening to God's Word. The Bible alone tells us of God's love in Christ the Savior — promised in the Old Testament and fulfilled in the New. To have Christ is to possess the highest wisdom and most priceless treasure. Then our lives will be truly happy regardless of our circumstances.

> Oh, blest the house, whate'er befall,
>> Where Jesus Christ is all in all!
> Yea, if he were not dwelling there,
>> How dark and poor and void it were!

6 **I have seen another evil under the sun, and it weighs heavily on men: ²God gives a man wealth, possessions and honor, so that he lacks nothing his heart desires, but God does not enable**

him to enjoy them, and a stranger enjoys them instead. This is meaningless, a grievous evil.

³A man may have a hundred children and live many years; yet no matter how long he lives, if he cannot enjoy his prosperity and does not receive proper burial, I say that a stillborn child is better off then he. ⁴It comes without meaning, it departs in darkness, and in darkness its name is shrouded. ⁵Though it never saw the sun or knew anything, it has more rest than does that man —⁶even if he lives a thousand years twice over but fails to enjoy his prosperity. Do not all go to the same place?

Unless God grants it, man can have *nothing*. Contrary to the American dream, there is no such creature as the "self-made" man. Regardless of how hard a person may work, it is God who "gives a man wealth, possessions and honor." Human effort or labor is merely the channel through which the Lord gives his "good and perfect gifts" (James 1:17). Luther describes it this way:

[All human activities] are our Lord God's masks; beneath these he chooses to be hidden and to do everything. Had Gideon not co-operated and taken the field against Midian, the Midianites would not have been defeated. Yet God was able to smite them without Gideon. No doubt he [God] could create children without man and woman, but he does not intend to do so. Rather he joins man and woman to make it look as if man and woman do the procreating. Yet he, hidden under this mask, is the one who does it. They say: God bestows every good thing; but you must "pitch in" and "take the bull by the horns," that is, you must work and supply God with a reason and a covering.[8]

In chapter 6 Solomon continues with this thought and expands on it. Not only must God give us what we have, but only he can enable us to enjoy it. *Possessing* things does not necessarily mean *enjoying* them. In fact, it often happens that the two do not go hand in hand. *Both* must come from God.

When people have possessions without enjoyment, it amounts to "another evil under the sun." A person's own fears can keep him from enjoying his possessions. Popular TV soap operas frequently depict this kind of individual. He's rich and powerful, but because of his selfishness and greed he's caught in one frustrating situation after another. The viewer rarely, if ever, sees him enjoying his vast possessions.

In real life, says Solomon, "a stranger" might end up enjoying another man's riches. Perhaps the wealthy man has no children. Perhaps some thief illegally gets hold of the money. However it comes about, it is God working behind the scenes. For one reason or another God is withholding enjoyment from the individual. He might withhold enjoyment because he wants the person to despair of riches and turn to God. Or he might withhold enjoyment as a judgment upon a wicked individual.

Even if this man were to have "a hundred children and live many years," his life would be sad. The hundred children may refer to his immediate children or include his grandchildren as well. In either case, he has a very large family. Back in ancient times large families were considered special blessings from God. Solomon mentions this in one of his Psalms, "Sons are a heritage from the Lord, children a reward from him. Like arrows in the hands of a warrior are sons born in one's youth. Blessed is the man whose quiver is full of them" (Psalm 127:3,4). In our day having many children is still a blessing from God, although some might not see it that way.

In verse 3 Solomon seems to be describing a wealthy man who puts off his own enjoyment and saves up for his children. They, however, are ungrateful and do not even honor their father with a proper burial, a matter always considered of importance in the Jewish community. In life and even in death the man is frustrated.

"A stillborn child is better off then he." This is a strong statement. In addition to the many children who die in miscarriage, we think of the millions who have been aborted in our country (a million and a half each year at the time of this writing). They are better off than the man who lives a miserable life without God and without being able to enjoy his gifts. "Thus the wicked begin their hell in this life," remarks Luther.

The stillborn child never enjoys the light of day, but passes from the darkness of his mother's womb to the darkness of the grave. If the child was named at all, the name quickly passes into obscurity, to be remembered only by his parents and, of course, the Lord. For all this sorrow connected with his existence, the stillborn child enjoys something the miserable adult doesn't have: rest. He is at rest from annoyance, toil, frustration, loneliness and lack of love.

When Solomon talks about the stillborn child, he is merely comparing its life "without meaning" to that of the man who is unable to enjoy his blessings. We can't draw any conclusions about what God does with all those unborn children whose lives are snuffed out. The Bible does not give us conclusive answers here. We must leave it in God's hands.

The oldest man ever to live was Methuselah. He reached the age of 969 (Genesis 5:27). Even if a man lives more than twice that long — "a thousand years twice over" — it's nothing but misery if God does not grant the gift of enjoyment.

One of the most written-about and talked-about expressions of our day is "quality-of-life." According to the quality-of-life outlook, certain lives are not worth living — the severely retarded, handicapped, senile, etc. People suffering from various disabilities supposedly miss out on so many of life's joys that they would be better off dead than alive. This type of thinking plays an important part in the abortion, infanticide and euthanasia controversies of our time.

Solomon is talking about something quite different from the modern idea of "quality." King Solomon does not see life's quality as depending upon a person's abilities or lack of them. Real quality-of-life comes only with a God-given contentment and thankfulness. Looking at it this way, often the wealthiest and most gifted people lack true quality-of-life, while the handicapped child of God lives a life of highest quality, in terms of happiness, contentment and hope.

The Teacher ends these verses with the question, "Do not all go to the same place?" Again he introduces death, that great equalizer. Whether your life has been happy or miserable, you still have to die.

> 7All man's efforts are for his mouth,
>   yet his appetite is never satisfied.
> 8What advantage has a wise man
>   over a fool?
> What does a poor man gain
>   by knowing how to conduct himself before others?
> 9Better what the eye sees
>   than the roving of the appetite.
> This too is meaningless,
>   a chasing after the wind.

In rapid-fire succession Solomon now rattles off a series of proverbs. Each relates in a different way to the meaninglessness of worldly wealth and activity. Together they capsulize everything Solomon has said about life under the sun.

"All a man's efforts are for his mouth. . . . " Everything a man does is for his self-preservation. We must remember that Solomon is describing life under the sun. Everyone looks out for himself. The term "mouth" can refer to all of man's physical needs, just as when Jesus talks about "daily bread" in the Lord's Prayer to signify whatever we need for our bodily welfare.

The attitude of looking out for oneself has almost become a religion in our "me generation." Advertising, television and popular wisdom bombard us with this theme. "You're number 1. . . . You deserve the best. . . . You owe it to yourself." And what is the result of all this emphasis? One's "appetite is never satisfied." We never have quite enough. We'll be happy (or so we think) *if* we get just one more raise or advancement or. . . .

Verse 8 consists of two questions. The first asks, "What advantage has a wise man over a fool?" The implied answer to this rhetorical question is, No advantage. For all his wisdom the wise man is still caught up in life's frustrations. Solomon immediately goes on to ask what a poor man gains from "knowing how to conduct himself before others." A poor man may conduct himself with wisdom, kindness and honesty only to be ignored or pushed aside in favor of a wealthy fool. Again, there seems to be no advantage. At least not under the sun.

"Better what the eye sees than the roving of the appetite." The word translated "appetite" here as in verse 7 literally means "soul." The soul, as one commentator puts it, is the "seat of the appetite." When we come right down to it, most of our "roving" desires are spiritual problems. Many married men are not satisifed with their own wives but, to use Jeremiah's expression, they are like "well-fed lusty stallions, each neighing for another man's wife" (Jeremiah 5:8). Others never have enough money, but always want more and more. Still others are never satisfied with their position in life. Such people are constantly restless. Beneath their restlessness lurks one of two problems: Either they are longing for

God (perhaps without even being aware of it) or they know about God but are dissatisfied with what he has given them. St. Augustine addressed both problems when he said, "The soul is restless till it rests in God"; and "He who is not satisfied with God alone is much too greedy." In either case, the problem is spiritual. It is a sickness of the soul.

Instead of letting our appetites roam, we should learn to control them. An old English proverb states, "A bird in the hand is worth two in the bush." This is what Solomon is saying with his words, "Better what the eye sees than the roving of the appetite." We can learn to appreciate what we have when we live in humble thankfulness for God's gifts.

> **10Whatever exists has already been named,**
> **and what man is has been known;**
> **no man can contend**
> **with one who is stronger than he.**
> **11The more the words,**
> **the less the meaning,**
> **and how does that profit anyone?**

Here Solomon introduces a variation on his words from the Prologue, "There is nothing new under the sun" (1:9). When it comes to human nature, man will always be man. "What man is has been known." The same weaknesses and sins that beset the ancients are still with us. The same desperate need for salvation from sin and death is still there. Man is still man.

Consequently it is as true today as it was in Solomon's day that "no man can contend with one who is stronger than he." The "one" most likely refers to God. How foolish it is to try to go against God's will. How foolish for modern man to think he can ignore the lessons of the past. God still punishes sin. Try as we might, we simply cannot overcome God and his plans. Rather than making a futile attempt to oppose God, we should trust him and stick close to him and his word.

Without God's word all human words are meaningless. We can talk all we want about the shape the world's in or about our personal lot in life, but it won't mean much of anything: "The more the words, the less the meaning." And it won't "profit" anyone.

[12]For who knows what is good for a man in life, during the few and meaningless days he passes through like a shadow? Who can tell him what will happen under the sun after he is gone?

A number of Scripture passages compare life to a shadow. One example is Psalm 144:4: "Man is like a breath; his days are like a fleeting shadow." Like a shadow that disappears into the darkness at the end of day, life under the sun quickly passes away. Life is short. There is little time to find out "what is good for a man in life." Who can tell him what is good? And "who can tell him what will happen under the sun after he is gone?"

Human wisdom has no certain answers to these questions. At best it can guess. Only the God who has created man knows what is best for man. Only that same eternal God can tell what the future holds.

The answers to these questions will take up the rest of Ecclesiastes. In the first half of the book the Teacher has dramatically depicted man's meaningless life under the sun. For the rest of the book he will emphasize the way life is meant to be lived — under God.

"Consider what God has done."

LIFE UNDER GOD
ECCLESIASTES 7:1-12:8

Unlike the Bibles we use today, the oldest copies of Scripture were not divided into chapters and verses. These divisions have been added to help people find passages more easily. Likewise, the section headings in this commentary are not part of the original Scriptures. They follow the headings which the New International Version translators inserted.

We have now finished six of Ecclesiastes' twelve chapters. And although these divisions were not in the original, there is at this half-way point a very obvious and strong shift in the book's emphasis. Previously Solomon has talked about God, but has emphasized the meaningless life under the sun. Now the emphasis is the other way around. He begins to stress how to avoid a meaningless existence by living a godly life.

If we were back in Jerusalem listening to Solomon, we might see him pause here. We detect a new energy in his speech, as he turns from asking questions to giving answers, and from desperate sorrow to definite solutions. He starts to talk about what is "good" and what is "better":

Wisdom

7 **A good name is better than fine perfume,**
   and the day of death better than the day of birth.
²It is better to go to a house of mourning
   than to go to a house of feasting,
for death is the destiny of every man;
   the living should take this to heart.

³Sorrow is better than laughter,
  because a sad face is good for the heart.
⁴The heart of the wise is in the house of mourning,
  but the heart of fools is in the house of pleasure.
⁵It is better to heed a wise man's rebuke
  than to listen to the song of fools.
⁶Like the crackling of thorns under the pot,
  so is the laughter of fools.
  This too is meaningless.

At first glance it seems that Solomon's tone is more pessimistic than ever. In one poetic verse after another he praises death, mourning, sorrow, and rebuke as being preferable to life, feasting, laughter and pleasure. As we look more closely, what he is doing becomes apparent. In effect, the king is saying, "If you want to live life as it should be lived, you must face it realistically, as it has become in this sinful world."

As a matter of fact, life is in such a sorry state that "the day of death [is] better than the day of birth." For the Christian, of course, death is the gate to Paradise. But even from a worldly standpoint, considering life's many sorrows, it would be better not to be than to be. King Solomon already expressed similar sentiments in 4:2. "And I declared that the dead . . . are happier than the living. . . . "

The first part of verse 1 — "a good name is better than fine perfume" — is merely there for the sake of comparison. *Just as* a good name is better than fine perfume, *so* the day of death is better than the day of birth. In the book of Proverbs Solomon also speaks of the value of a good reputation: "A good name is more desirable than riches" (22:1). In comparing one's name or reputation to perfume, Solomon is not just pointing out how pleasing a good name is. He is also making a play on the Hebrew words for name (*shem*) and perfume, or oil (*shemen*). This type of play on words is common in Hebrew poetry, much as in English. Solomon uses the same expression in the Song of Songs: "Your name is like perfume" (Song of Songs 1:3).

Getting back to the main point, Solomon compares the "house of mourning" with the "house of feasting." He tells why it is better to visit a funeral parlor than a banquet hall. "For death is the destiny of every man; the living should take this to heart." To examine death makes us realize how frail and brief life is. It also moves us to think about the cause of death. "Sin entered the world through one man, and death through sin, and in this way death came to all men, because all sinned" (Romans 5:12). And it leads us to reflect on the only solution and escape from death. "Where sin increased, grace increased all the more, so that, just as sin reigned in death, so also grace might reign through righteousness to bring eternal life through Jesus Christ our Lord" (Romans 5:21). Through Christ's perfect life, sacrificial death on the cross and resurrection from the dead, we have forgiveness and eternal life.

Solomon continues. It is better to enter into life's sorrow than to try to run away from it. We should share in the grief of others. This was the way of our Savior. He was, in the Prophet Isaiah's words, "a man of sorrows, and familiar with suffering," and "he took up our infirmities and carried our sorrows" (Isaiah 53:3,4).

King Solomon did not have the New Testament believer's insight into all these truths. Even Isaiah lived two centuries after Solomon. Yet the Teacher certainly knew of the reality of sin and of the promised Savior.

People who do not share the believer's hope will try to avoid sorrow and death. This philosophy wants to forget about life's sadness and live for the pleasures of the moment. Solomon himself had tried that route. Our culture has taken it a step farther. It attempts to shove death itself out of the realm of reality. Violence on television gives the impression that somehow death isn't quite real. The good guys knock off the crooks like flies and hardly give it a thought. After all, everyone knows it's only make-believe. Meanwhile the real thing takes place everywhere, often without the dying person's family anywhere around.

"Fools" is the label Solomon gives to people who don't want to face life as it is. A fool is of no help to himself or to others. Instead of dealing with evil and trying to correct it, he'll joke about it or heap empty words of praise on the wrongdoer. This is "the song of fools." Even though criticism may hurt and bring sadness, "it is better to heed a wise man's rebuke."

The foolish attempt to laugh one's way through life is futile. It's like making a fire of thorns which might give off a loud and crackling sound, but never lasts long. Such is "the laughter of fools." It is empty, meaningless.

At times troubles become so pressing that even the most foolish individual can no longer avoid life's serious side. Pain, remarked C. S. Lewis, is God's "megaphone." Trouble may prove a priceless blessing, if in his need a person comes to rely on God. Sometimes entire societies are shaken out of their complacency. In our troubled age many people are searching for spiritual values.

> **7 Extortion turns a wise man into a fool,**
> **and a bribe corrupts the heart.**
> **8 The end of a matter is better than its beginning,**
> **and patience is better than pride.**
> **9 Do not be quickly provoked in your spirit,**
> **for anger resides in the lap of fools.**
> **10 Do not say, "Why were the old days better than these?"**
> **For it is not wise to ask such questions.**

Just as a fool can sometimes become wise, the same can also happen in reverse. Don't be proud of your godliness or wisdom. You might be ripe for a fall. Perhaps you are in a position where you handle a lot of money or have become wealthy. Then heed the Psalmist's words, "Though your riches increase, do not set your heart on them" (Psalm 62:10). The temptation to cheat others, or to give or take bribes, can be the downfall of any man or woman.

Hand in hand with temptations of worldly success goes impatience. We often become impatient when things don't progress as quickly as we would like. So Solomon reminds us, "The end of a matter is better than its beginning." That is, a finished task is better than one left incomplete and therefore useless. Solomon is saying, "Don't go jumping from one project to the next in the hope of instant success." Commentator C. Wolff remarks on this passage:

> There are, to be sure, proud spirits who believe themselves capable of accomplishing great things and whose brain is feverish with grandiose projects. . . . They start many projects, but when their work does not progress with the desired ease and speed, they quickly tire and their work remains unfinished. By contrast, God usually begins his works in a small way and has them develop slowly midst many difficulties, so that man may learn the patience and perseverance which the Scriptures ascribe to God in the achieving of his works. "The kingdom of heaven is like a mustard seed, which a man took and planted in his field. . . . the smallest of all your seeds" (Matthew 13:31,32). Jesus began his kingdom by sending twelve Galilean fishermen out into the world.[9]

Not only do we need to learn patience, we also need to avoid anger. From impatience flows anger. We human beings tend to become irritated when our plans don't work out. This is another mark of the fool. The wise man understands that God is in control. We must entrust our work to him and await his time.

In the first nine verses of chapter 7, the Teacher has made seven comparisons using the word "better." In verse 10 he introduces an eighth comparison, in which we should *not* use the word. "Do not say, 'Why were the old days better than these?' " Most of us like to talk about the "good old days." Whether we are referring to the days of our childhood or when our grandparents were young or some other century, such comparisons are "not wise." Why not? Simply because the old days were not better. Since the Fall, the days have always been evil. In some ways our age might be much worse than another. In other ways our age may be better. For instance, while today's mass media have helped spread many ungodly ideas, they have also helped Christians to share the gospel.

Just as every age is full of wickedness, God's goodness also remains from one age to the next. In this respect *no* day has ever been better than today. God's Word is there for us to learn and to live. Scripture declares, "Today, if you hear his [God's] voice, do not harden your hearts" (Hebrews 4:7).

We want to become aware of the dangers of our times. Let's also look for the special opportunities we have to serve God.

Impatience, anger, desire for worldly success, longing for the old days — all come from the fool's desire to make a heaven on earth and to escape life's sorrows. How much better to search for a real treasure, godly wisdom:

> 11 Wisdom, like an inheritance, is a good thing
>   and benefits those who see the sun.
> 12 Wisdom is a shelter
>   as money is a shelter,

> but the advantage of knowledge is this:
>   that wisdom preserves the life of its possessor.
> [13] Consider what God has done:
>   Who can straighten
>   what he has made crooked?
> [14] When times are good, be happy;
>   but when times are bad, consider:
> God has made the one
>   as well as the other.
> Therefore, a man cannot discover
>   anything about his future.

The Teacher compares wisdom with an inheritance. Both are good. Both benefit people "who see the sun," that is, who live on earth. They serve as shelters. Money in the bank or in an insurance policy provides shelter from financial disaster when there is sickness or death in a family.

But wisdom has an "advantage" over money. It "preserves the life of its possessor." Here one might think of the advantages of a good education or knowledge of some trade. The person who possesses the right skills is able to find a job and make a living.

There is another wisdom which goes beyond this and preserves one's life forever. It comes from knowing the Holy Scriptures, "which are able to make you wise for salvation through faith in Christ Jesus" (2 Timothy 3:15).

The right kind of wisdom leads us to "consider what God has done." We come to see that everything is in his hands. No one can "straighten what he has made crooked." No one can change what God ordains.

It is wisdom, then, to accept what God sends. He sends bad times as well as good. When life is pleasant we can be happy and thankful, recognizing even temporary blessings as gifts from a loving God. When troubles come we can accept them as well, trusting that they, too, are for our good. We can go even further than accepting our troubles. We can rejoice in them. "Consider it pure joy, my brothers, whenever you face trials of many kinds, because you know that the testing of your faith develops perseverance" (James 1:2,3).

We have no way of knowing how long the good or bad times will last. Only the almighty God knows. And he "works out everything in conformity with the purpose of his will" (Ephesians 1:11), namely, his plan of salvation through Christ. In good and bad times alike he simply wants us to trust him.

The Bible defines faith as "being sure of what we hope for and certain of what we do not see" (Hebrews 11:1). Solomon is urging faith. We need faith because we can't see what lies ahead in our lives. We also need faith because it often seems as if God's goodness and justice are nowhere to be found in this world.

> 15In this meaningless life of mine I have seen both of these:
> a righteous man perishing in his righteousness,
> and a wicked man living long in his wickedness.
> 16Do not be overrighteous,
> neither be overwise —
> why destroy yourself?
> 17Do not be overwicked,
> and do not be a fool —
> why die before your time?
> 18It is good to grasp the one
> and not let go of the other.
> The man who fears God will avoid all extremes.

When the Teacher speaks of his "meaningless life" we should remember everything behind that word "meaningless." Life is fleeting, like a breath. In our short lives we lack the time and perspective to see the entire picture of God's eternal plans. Consequently, it frequently appears that God has lost control. Life seems topsy-turvy. The righteous man perishes; the wicked thrives in his wickedness. This is a subject Solomon touched on earlier in Ecclesiastes (4:1), and he will return to it again (8:14). It is a subject that often bothers God's people. It troubled Job in his suffering. It bothered the Psalmist Asaph a great deal, who wrote,

> For I envied the arrogant,
>> when I saw the prosperity of the wicked.
> They have no struggles;
>> their bodies are healthy and strong. . . .
> They say, "How can God know?
>> Does the Most High have knowledge?"
> This is what the wicked are like —
>> always carefree, they increase in wealth.
> Surely in vain I have kept my heart pure.
>> in vain I washed my hands in innocence.
> All day long I have been plagued;
>> I have been punished every morning. . . .
>> (Psalm 73)

Following his observations about injustice, Solomon's next remark might appear somewhat cynical: "Do not be overrighteous, neither be overwise — why destroy yourself?" What he's saying is: Don't be self-righteous. In Jesus' words, "Why do you look at the speck of sawdust in your brother's eye and pay no attention to the plank in your own eye?" (Matthew 7:3) To be sure, the unrighteous do flourish in the world. But before getting too upset about it, we should look at our own lives and say, "If God would have punished me for everything I've done, I'd be much worse off than I am." There are more than enough wicked and foolish deeds in our past to keep us from being "overrighteous" or "overwise."

People who are too righteous or too wise might end up destroying themselves. They become so rigid that they invite rebellion and disaster. Parents, teachers and government lawmakers must learn to temper justice with mercy. There are times to wink at a bit of foolishness.

The extreme opposite of being overrighteous is being "overwicked." Some might foolishly conclude that because the world is so wicked anyway, they may as well indulge themselves. Solomon responds to that attitude by saying, "Why die before your time?"

Even if some overly wicked people manage to escape the heavy hand of the law in this life, they still have to face God's justice. Those who boldly rebel against God's laws will eventually suffer God's wrath. The Psalmist Asaph came to recognize this. "How suddenly are they destroyed, completely swept away by terrors!" (Psalm 73:19)

The Teacher instructs us to avoid extremes. Verse 18 literally says, "The man who fears God will follow them both." The idea is that of taking the middle road between two extremes. We come to know this proper way as we regularly study the Scriptures and then apply them in the hard school of experience.

> 19Wisdom makes one wise man more powerful
>   than ten rulers in a city.
> 20There is not a righteous man on earth
>   who does what is right and never sins.
> 21Do not pay attention to every word people say,
>   or you may hear your servant cursing you —
> 22for you know in your heart
>   that many times you yourself have cursed others.

The person who has wisdom makes a good ruler. He avoids extremes and is able to balance justice with compassion. This makes him powerful and more effective "than ten rulers in a city." In his early years as king, Solomon had been such a ruler. Other kings and queens respected him because of his ability to rule wisely.

74

One of the prayers in *The Lutheran Hymnal* includes the request, "Grant health and prosperity to all that are in authority . . . and endue them with grace to rule after thy good pleasure, to the maintenance of righteousness and to the hindrance and punishment of wickedness. . . . " Exceptionally wise rulers are a rare blessing to their cities and lands. We should often pray that God will give our leaders such wisdom.

One characteristic of wise rulers is a keen understanding of human nature. They realize that "there is not a righteous man on earth who does what is right and never sins." If a ruler has too high a view of human nature, he will make one of two mistakes. He will be overly strict and unwilling to overlook common human frailties. Or he will be too lenient and let the people run rampant on the assumption that they will naturally do what is right.

The words of verse 20 occur elsewhere in Scripture. Solomon used almost the exact wording in his prayer at the dedication of the temple. "There is no one who does not sin" (1 Kings 8:46). He then went on to ask God, "Forgive your people." St. Paul paraphrases verse 20 in Romans 3:10, "As it is written: 'There is no one righteous, not even one.' " Paul proceeds to demonstrate man's complete inability to save himself and his complete dependence on the grace of God. "This righteousness from God comes through faith in Jesus Christ to all who believe" (Romans 3:22). Solomon, too, wants us to realize our complete dependence on God in every area of life.

Because of man's sinfulness, a wise man will learn not to be overly sensitive to what others say. "Do not pay attention to every word people say, or you may hear your servant cursing you." After all, Solomon adds, you yourself have often done the same thing! How often haven't you cursed others — that is, belittled them or spoken evil against them.

Given man's sinful condition and tendency to criticize, you are likely to hear some unfavorable remarks if you listen in on what others are saying about you. The better people know you, the better they know your faults. Someone has observed, "No man is a hero to his valet."

²³All this I tested by wisdom and I said,
   "I am determined to be wise" —
   but this was beyond me.
²⁴Whatever wisdom may be,
   it is far off and most profound —
   who can discover it?
²⁵So I turned my mind to understand,
   to investigate and to search our wisdom and the scheme
      of things
   and to understand the stupidity of wickedness
   and the madness of folly.
²⁶I find more bitter than death
   the woman who is a snare,
   whose heart is a trap
   and whose hands are chains.
The man who pleases God will escape her,
   but the sinner she will ensnare.

Early in the book of Ecclesiastes Solomon had shown that worldly wisdom is meaningless (1:12-18). Although he had attained much wisdom, it brought nothing but sorrow and grief. What sort of wisdom is the Teacher talking about now, when he says that the attainment of wisdom is "beyond" him? With his shift in emphasis to life under God, it's likely that he is speaking of godly wisdom.

In one sense, of course, this wisdom is not beyond people. True wisdom resides in God's Word. According to Deuteronomy 30:11-14, God's Word "is not too difficult. . . . No, the word is very near you; it is in your mouth and in your heart so you may obey it." God's Word is as clear as a "lamp" and "light" (Psalm 119:105).

That doesn't mean we will always understand everything in the Bible. For example, the Bible clearly teaches that God is triune — one God in three Persons. We cannot understand the Trinity even though we know it is what the Scriptures teach. What is "beyond" us, then, is not the ability to read and know what the Bible teaches. Rather, it is the fact that many scriptural truths surpass our ability to reason them out.

There is something else involved here, too. Solomon is saying that we human beings will never exhaust all there is to know. Nobody reaches the point where he knows it all. Even if we get to know a tremendous amount of information, we still must learn to apply it practically!

So while the wisdom of God is accessible ("the word is near you"), at the same time it is inexhaustible ("beyond" you). Let's never stop studying and applying the Word of God. King Solomon's statement about wisdom being "profound" (literally, "deep") finds another parallel in the writings of the Apostle Paul. "Oh, the depth of the riches of the wisdom and knowledge of God!" (Romans 11:33)

It's sad that so few take the time to probe the depths of those riches. So many are satisfied with so little. Some think of themselves as being Bible experts if they know the Ten Commandments and the Lord's Prayer. Others have little or no time for seeking out godly wisdom. They are too concerned about worldly wisdom.

Solomon continued "to investigate and to search out wisdom . . . to understand the stupidity of wickedness and the madness of folly." Here he is sharing his observations with us. One of those observations has to do with the danger of a woman whose "heart is a trap and whose hands are chains."

Because this passage about a woman suddenly appears in the middle of Solomon's discussion of wisdom, some commentators think the evil woman symbolizes false wisdom which leads people astray. It's true that in the book of Proverbs Solomon personifies wisdom as a woman. "Wisdom calls aloud in the street, she raises her voice in the public squares" (Proverbs 1:20). Nevertheless, in Ecclesiastes 7 the Teacher is speaking of practical matters from daily life, such as the importance of avoiding extremes (7:16-18). Most likely Solomon is describing a woman who does not keep a proper balance in her relationships.

Contrary to Scripture, she may lack "a gentle and quiet spirit" (1 Peter 3:4) and be domineering. Perhaps she is "overrighteous" or "overwicked." She might be a gossip or a woman who wants to spend all her time in a "house of feasting." Whatever her faults, she is a snare "more bitter than death."

Solomon speaks from experience. His wives had led him astray and had made a fool of him. Luther offers these words on the passage, "Those who are wise in the Word of God run away from these snares but not from the female sex." In other words, don't avoid women, but just the wrong kind of women.

²⁷"Look," says the Teacher, "this is what I have discovered:
  "Adding one thing to another to discover the scheme
    of things —
²⁸while I was still searching
  but not finding —
I found one ⌊upright⌋ man among a thousand,
  but not one ⌊upright⌋ woman among them all.
²⁹This only have I found:
  God made mankind upright,
  but men have gone in search of many schemes."

"Speaking of wisdom," continues Solomon, "here's something I discovered while I was searching under the sun for the scheme of things. . . . " What the king happened upon was this: "I found one [upright] man among a thousand, but not one [upright] woman among them all." The brackets in the translation indicate the word "upright" is not in the original Hebrew. Literally Solomon says, "I found one man . . .but not one woman. . . . " What kind of man or woman does he mean? The translators added the word "upright" because it fits the context and is used in the next verse. The translators might have inserted the word "wise" instead of "upright," since Solomon has been discussing wisdom throughout this chapter.

When he alludes to a thousand women, is Solomon thinking of his harem of seven hundred wives and three hundred concubines? Perhaps after his bitter experiences with them the king had reached the conclusion that not one of them was wise or upright. When he mentions one man in a thousand, maybe he is referring to some of the great leaders of God's people — men like Abraham, Joseph, Moses.

Earlier in the chapter Solomon had spoken of qualities which are necessary for a wise leader. According to God's inspired Word — of which Ecclesiastes is a part — men are to be the leaders in home (1 Peter 3:1-7) and church (1 Corinthians 14:33-36). Even among men wise leadership is a rare gift. Perhaps one in a thousand have it. Solomon is simply pointing out how rare a truly upright or wise person is — whether that person be male or female.

The king goes on to state that all people, both men and women, share a common problem. All are under God's judgment against sin. Although in the beginning "God made mankind upright," all of us have gone astray. We all have spent our time working on our own "schemes" rather than following God's will. As in many other passages, the Apostle

James reflects Solomon's thoughts here. "When tempted, no one should say, 'God is tempting me.' For God cannot be tempted by evil, but each one is tempted when, by his own evil desire, he is dragged away and enticed" (James 1:13,14). How often haven't we followed our own evil desires and schemes rather than the wisdom of God's Word!

This brings the longest chapter in Ecclesiastes to a close. Solomon ends it as he began. We must face the reality that we live in a fallen world filled with death and sin.

Now the Teacher is about to turn to the next lesson for godly living under the sun, Obey the King. But first, one more verse about wisdom —

8   **Who is like the wise man?**
    Who knows the explanation of things?
    Wisdom brightens a man's face
    and changes its hard appearance.

Here Solomon praises the wonderful gift of wisdom. His questions in this verse are rhetorical, not really expecting an answer. He's saying something like this: "Who can compare to the wise man? Who knows the explanation of things as he does? Wisdom makes for a happy person." We cannot help comparing this joyful wisdom with that empty worldly wisdom which brings nothing but "much sorrow" (1:18). True wisdom is a bottomless treasure. It is there for the taking in God's Word.

The really wise person not only comes to know "things," but also their "explanation." Many people have a lot of facts at their finger tips or degrees behind their names, but do not have a real grasp of what it all means.

Not so with the wise man. He knows the explanation of things. He knows that behind life's complexities and seeming injustices, God is at work. He understands that God is using everything for the good of his people. The wise man understands all this and he confidently places his life into God's loving hands.

Every field of learning takes on a new light when viewed in this way. History, for instance, becomes more than the recounting of the rise and fall of nations. It is the story of the Almighty's blessings and judgments upon the nations as he carries out his plans.

No wonder godly wisdom "brightens a man's face and changes its hard appearance." Solomon's father David put it this way, "The precepts of the Lord are right, giving joy to the heart. The commands of the Lord are radiant, giving light to the eyes" (Psalm 19:8). But how does this fit with Solomon's words in chapter 7, "Sorrow is better than laughter, because a sad face is good for the heart"? The fact is that the Christian is both — "sorrowful, yet always rejoicing" (2 Corinthians 6:10). True wisdom leads to sorrow over our sins and over the world's wretched, lost condition. At the same time it leads to happiness, not in the shallow pleasures this world can offer, but in God's solutions to sin and death. We are always joyful because of our Savior Jesus Christ.

While the unbelieving world is losing itself in feasting and laughter, the wise person is sad. He knows the end of such folly. On the other hand, when everything seems to be going against him, he can rejoice. He knows God is in charge. When Stephen, the first Christian martyr, was put on trial for his life his face was radiant "like the face of an angel" (Acts 6:15). He was soon to meet his God.

Obey the King

2Obey the king's command, I say, because you took an oath before God. 3Do not be in a hurry to leave the king's presence. Do not stand up for a bad cause, for he will do whatever he pleases.

⁴Since a king's word is supreme, who can say to him, "What are you doing?"
>⁵Whoever obeys his command will come to no harm,
>and the wise heart will know the proper time
>and procedure.
>⁶For there is a proper time and procedure for every matter,
>though a man's misery weighs heavily upon him.

Because Solomon speaks in general terms in Ecclesiastes, some passages lend themselves to several applications. This is such a passage. The king he speaks of could be either an earthly ruler or the King of kings, that is, God. Since the Hebrew language makes no distinction between small and capital letters, it's up to the translators to decide on that.

The idea of God as King was nothing new at Solomon's time. In several psalms David had spoken in that manner. For instance, in Psalm 5:2 he wrote, "Listen to my cry for help, my King and my God, for to you I pray." In my opinion Solomon has such a passage in mind.

Actually, obedience to God and to human government go hand in hand. The second follows from the first. Luther points out, "Political obedience is included in obedience to God." The Lord expects his people to respect government authority. "Everyone must submit himself to the governing authorities, for there is no authority except that which God has established. The authorities that exist have been established by God" (Romans 13:1-7).

If Solomon is speaking directly of God, then God and "king" in verse 2 are synonymous. And the "oath before God" would be the allegiance that God's people promise him. In Deuteronomy 29:12 Moses spoke of such an oath between God and his nation Israel: "You are standing here in order to enter into a covenant with the Lord your God, a covenant the Lord is making with you this day and sealing with an oath." Later, at the time of Nehemiah (about 445 B.C.), the Jews again made "an oath to follow the Law of God" (Nehemiah 10:29).

Loyalty to God is the best foundation for loyalty to the government. When Solomon became king, the people "made sacrifices to the Lord. . . . all the officers and mighty men, as well as all of King David's sons, pledged their submission to King Solomon" (1 Chronicles 29:21,24). Today American citizens "pledge allegiance to the flag of the United States of America and to the republic for which it stand, one nation under God."

It is difficult for us to appreciate the injunction, "Do not be in a hurry to leave the king's presence." In ancient times people stood in awe of their rulers. One did not enter or leave a king's presence without his permission. The expression "to leave the king's presence" was another way of saying "to leave without permission." Simply to turn one's back on a king and walk out was a terrible insult to the monarch. To do so would invite almost certain death.

To leave God's presence is nothing short of forsaking him. Genesis 4:16 uses a similar expression when it says that Cain "went out from the Lord's presence." To turn against God invites certain and eternal death.

Nor dare we turn against our earthly government. "He who rebels against the authority is rebelling against what God has instituted, and those who do so will bring judgment on themselves" (Romans 13:2). Only if the earthly authority orders us to go contrary to the higher authority of God should we resist it.

"Do not stand up for a bad cause, for he will do whatever he pleases" is another warning against opposing the King. Again Paul's words in Romans 13 reflect Solomon's: "If you do wrong, be afraid, for he [the governing authority] does not bear the sword for nothing." Of course only God the

King completely does "whatever he pleases." Worldly rulers have great power — including the power to punish law-breakers — but it is nothing compared to the Almighty's.

Living in a democracy and in a society where authority frequently is more suspected than respected, twentieth-century Americans might be more inclined to ask of their government leaders, "What are you doing?" Indeed, as good citizens in a democracy (government by the people) it is our obligation. But we must remember, "A king's [or, the King's] word is supreme." We are in no position to question God's Word. "Woe to him who quarrels with his Maker" (Isaiah 45:9). Nor ought we speak against those laws of the land which are just and beneficial.

"Do you want to be free from fear of the one in authority?" asked St. Paul, "Then do what is right and he will commend you. For he is God's servant to do you good" (Romans 13:3,4). In King Solomon's words, you "will come to no harm." If a government functions the way it should, it will punish the evildoer and protect the law-abiding citizen. If not, God will bring that government down in his good time. Governments which foster injustice are sowing the seeds of their own destruction.

The "wise heart" knows "the proper time and procedure." The wise person knows that when God sees fit justice will be done. Meanwhile, it can be difficult waiting. A man's misery under an oppressive government might "weigh heavily upon him."

But there is a time for everything (3:1), and at the proper time God will rescue his people. If that deliverance doesn't come in this life, it will in the next. In the end God saves us from every evil, including those spiritual forces which would oppress and destroy our soul. Once more we quote from St. Paul. Imprisoned, awaiting trial and expecting the death sentence, Paul wrote, "The Lord will rescue me from every evil attack and will bring me safely to his heavenly kingdom" (2 Timothy 4:18). The King is in control.

> **⁷Since no man knows the future,**
>   **who can tell him what is to come?**
> **⁸No man has power over the wind to contain it;**
>   **so no one has power over the day of his death.**
> **As no one is discharged in time of war,**
>   **so wickedness will not release those who practice it.**

We can be sure that in the end God will use everything for our good. But in this life we never can be sure of what is coming next. God withholds that information from us, and no one else can give it. Since that's the case, we should be content, live one day at a time, and entrust everything to God.

We might mention in passing that Scripture clearly opposes attempts to discover the future from the stars (horoscopes and astrology) or from fortunetellers. The Prophet Isaiah ridiculed those who look to the stars for guidance. "Let your astrologers come forward, those stargazers who make predictions month by month, let them save you from what is coming upon you. . . . They cannot even save themselves" (Isaiah 47:13,14). And speaking of those who turn to fortunetellers who try to consult with spirits of the dead, Isaiah states, "When men tell you to consult mediums and spiritists, who whisper and mutter, should not a people inquire of their God? Why consult the dead on behalf of the living? To the law and to the testimony! If they do not speak according to this word, they have no light of dawn" (Isaiah 8:19,20). Any attempt to predict the future that is not in line with God's Word is forbidden.

Human beings can no more determine the time of their own death than they can control which way the wind blows. Even a suicide attempt will fail if God decides to stop it. As

Jesus said, "The wind blows wherever it pleases" (John 3:8). Since the Hebrew word for wind and spirit is the same, Solomon's statement about the wind might also be translated, "No man has power over his spirit to retain it," that is, to hold it from leaving the body at the moment of death.

Although man can neither predict nor control the events of his life, he can be sure of one thing. Sooner or later he is going to die. Just as no soldier is "discharged in time of war," so no one escapes the final struggle of death. For the wicked there is no peace. "Wickedness will not release those who practice it." They must face the consequences — if not in this life than before God who "will call the past to account" (3:15).

⁹All this I saw, as I applied my mind to everything done under the sun. There is a time when a man lords it over others to his own hurt. ¹⁰Then too, I saw the wicked buried — those who used to come and go from the holy place and receive praise in the city where they did this. This too is meaningless.

¹¹When the sentence for a crime is not quickly carried out, the hearts of the people are filled with schemes to do wrong. ¹²Although a wicked man commits a hundred crimes and still lives a long time, I know that it will go better with God-fearing men, who are reverent before God. ¹³Yet because the wicked do not fear God, it will not go well with them, and their days will not lengthen like a shadow.

¹⁴There is something else meaningless that occurs on earth: righteous men who get what the wicked deserve, and wicked men who get what the righteous deserve. This too, I say, is meaningless. ¹⁵So I commend the enjoyment of life, because nothing is better for a man under the sun than to eat and drink and be glad. Then joy will accompany him in his work all the days of the life God has given him under the sun.

In this section Solomon returns to several topics he has already introduced: oppression, wrongdoing, God's final justice, and the enjoyment of life.

86

The first verse might refer to a person oppressing others "to his own hurt," or, as a footnote in the New International Version (NIV) indicates, "to their hurt." In the former reading the verse speaks of justice eventually catching up with the oppressor. In the latter it speaks of harm done to others. The actual meaning is "a man lords it over a man to his hurt." "His" could refer to either party. Both readings fit what Solomon has been saying.

Verse 10 also speaks of the wicked, this time of their burial. It describes them as "those who used to come and go from the holy place," namely, God's house. Again there are two possible understandings for the verse. Either these wicked people "used to . . . receive praise" or they "are forgotten" (footnote). The first points to the unfairness of life under the sun: even in the house of God the wicked receive praise. The other points to the end result of their life: they are forgotten. In the words of Psalm 34:16, "The face of the Lord is against those who do evil, to cut off the memory of them from the earth." God will see to it that the wicked are forgotten or, if they are remembered, people will not honor them but will want to forget them. Again, either understanding of the verse fits the context of Solomon's thought.

Throughout this commentary I've pointed out footnotes in the NIV translation for those readers who may have noted them while studying the Bible. Since we've just encountered two consecutive verses with them, this might be a good place for a comment. Some of the different readings are based on the different possible translations from the original language into English. Others are based on slight variations in the ancient hand-written copies of Scripture. In either case these variations ought not disturb us. They do not affect any teaching of Scripture. Moreover, the Bible — both Old and New Testaments — has been passed down through the ages with amazing accuracy, more so than any other ancient book. Referring to the Old Testament in particular, one scholar sums it up, "[It] may be safely said that no other work of antiquity has been so accurately transmitted."[10]

Footnotes aside, Solomon proceeds to explain why the wicked often get away with as much as they do: "When the sentence for a crime is not quickly carried out, the hearts of the people are filled with schemes to do wrong." These words have a very modern ring to them. Today we hear many voices calling for stricter and quicker sentences for lawbreakers. A sluggish judicial system not only encourages those bent on evil. It is also a temptation to others to think, "Why should I try to do what is right?"

Although they might be tempted, "God-fearing men" have strong motives for fighting the temptation to indulge themselves in evil. For one thing, they know that whatever the wicked get away with is short-lived. God notices. And God punishes. Before the wicked accomplish half of what they set out to do, their end will suddenly come. Their lives will not stretch out like a shadow lengthening late in the day.

Besides understanding the futility of wickedness, God's people "are reverent" before him. They stand in awe of God and have too much respect for him to sin against him willfully.

In trying to serve God, sometimes the righteous appear to get what the wicked deserve. And the wicked are rewarded. Godly men like Stephen and Paul are put to death, while tyrants are honored and praised.

Because we live in a fallen world, this should not surprise us. Nor should we be bitter. The only person ever to lead a completely perfect life was the most persecuted of all. And he gives us this assurance, "If the world hates you, keep in mind that it hated me first. If you belonged to the world it would love you as its own. As it is, you do not belong to the world, but I have chosen you out of the world. That is why the world hates you" (John 15:18,19).

Commenting on why Solomon keeps returning to the subject of life's unfairness, Luther says, "This is said so often so that we might instruct our hearts and teach good people what the world is, a raging and ungrateful beast, . . . one that cannot do anything but to exalt the wicked and oppress the godly. We should not expect anything else."

Each time Solomon brings up the topic of injustice, he does so from a slightly different angle and with a somewhat different lesson to teach. Here he uses it as a reason to "commend the enjoyment of life." You're not going to change the world. Do the best you can to live your faith and share it. And enjoy the gifts God gives you. As you enjoy them, think of how good God is. Then you'll find satisfaction in your work during the time God gives you under the sun.

16When I applied my mind to know wisdom and to observe man's labor on earth — his eyes not seeing sleep day or night —17then I saw all that God has done. No one can comprehend what goes on under the sun. Despite all his efforts to search it out, man cannot discover its meaning. Even if a wise man claims he knows, he cannot really comprehend it.

"Anxiety: Millions are tormented by this disorder." So says a modern newspaper headline. The article goes on to relate an example: "The 37-year-old mother lay in bed, unable to sleep, shaking with shivers that blankets couldn't calm. It was her first anxiety attack."[11] As Solomon's words show, the problem is nothing new. Generations of people have spent countless sleepless nights and troubled days, yet to no avail. Life remains as toilsome and incomprehensible as ever. This is part of God's doing. He has subjected the fallen world to a condition of frustration.

Some philosophers might claim to have solved the riddle of life. But what have the world's wise men ever been able to tell us about the origin, purpose and destiny of life under the sun? "The wisdom of the wise will perish," declares God, "the intelligence of the intelligent will vanish" (Isaiah 29:14). The fact that Solomon uses the phrase "under the sun" indicates that he is referring to such worldly wisdom rather than godly wisdom.

No human being on his own can discover life's meaning. God alone can reveal it.

A Common Destiny for All

9 So I reflected on all this and concluded that the righteous and the wise and what they do are in God's hands, but no man knows whether love or hate awaits him. ²All share a common destiny — the righteous and the wicked, the good and the bad, the clean and the unclean, those who offer sacrifices and those who do not.

> As it is with the good man,
>   so with the sinner;
> as it is with those who take oaths,
>   so with those who are afraid to take them.

In the last couple chapters the Teacher has been showing how to live a godly life under the sun. He has shown that the godly life includes facing life realistically (chapter 7). It also includes obedience to the King and respect for authority (chapter 8). For most of chapter 9 Solomon emphasizes that to live as we should, we must constantly be aware of the brevity of earthly life.

"The righteous and the wise and what they do are in God's hands." What comfort this short sentence contains for believers! By nature we are all unrighteous and foolish, bent on leaving the King's presence and following our own schemes.

But God has given us the gifts of forgiveness and wisdom through his Word. He has made us his own people, of whom Jesus says, "I give them eternal life, and they shall never perish; no one can snatch them out of my hand" (John 10:28). It is good to know we are in God's hands.

In this life one can never be certain "whether love or hate awaits him." In previous chapters Solomon has made it clear enough that the way a person is treated in this world is no indication of his standing with God. Moreover, the Scriptures teach us that as God's people we can frequently expect the world's hatred. God himself permits it to come our way. To what measure and at what times we'll experience hatred or love, only God knows.

But of this we can be sure: "All share a common destiny." All are going to die. The righteous, the wicked, the good, the bad, the clean, the unclean, those who offer sacrifices and those who don't, saints and sinners, those who take oaths and those who are afraid to — everyone will die.

Solomon's all-inclusive list is self-explanatory, but a few of the terms call for some comment. The "clean" are those who kept the many Old Testament ceremonial laws, given to Moses at Mt. Sinai along with the Ten Commandments. These regulations (discussed in the book of Leviticus) included washing, eating the right (clean) foods, and making distinctions between infectious and non-infectious diseases. Leviticus 13:38-46 furnishes an example:

> When a man or woman has white spots on the skin, the priest is to examine them, and if the spots are dull white, it is a harmless rash that has broken out on the skin; that person is clean. . . . [But] if the swollen sore on his head or forehead is reddish-white like an infectious skin disease, the man is diseased and is unclean. . . .

The person with such an infectious disease must wear torn clothes, let his hair be unkempt, cover the lower part of his face and cry out, "Unclean! Unclean!" As long as he has the infection he remains unclean. He must live alone; he must live outside the camp.

Solomon also refers to "those who offer sacrifices and those who do not." The Old Testament ceremonial laws called for various sacrifices on different occasions. Pious Jews faithfully offered these sacrifices during the fourteen centuries between Moses and the destruction of the second temple in A.D. 70. For example, when Jesus was a baby Joseph and Mary took him to the temple to consecrate him to the Lord and "to offer a sacrifice in keeping with what is said in the Law of the Lord: 'a pair of doves or two young pigeons' " (Luke 2:22-24).

King Solomon also mentions those who take oaths and "those who are afraid to take them." The Teacher previously discussed the subject of oaths in Ecclesiastes 5:4-7.

By listing all these different kinds of people, Solomon is alluding to every kind of reputation among men. Some are outcasts (the unclean); some are respected (the good man and those who offer sacrifices); some are looked down on (the sinner); some are considered bold (those who take oaths); others seem timid (those who are afraid to take oaths). Regardless of their standing among men, all these people are brought to the same level in death. Then the real sorting out begins, as they stand before the judgment throne of God.

³**This is the evil in everything that happens under the sun: The same destiny overtakes all. The hearts of men, moreover, are full of evil and there is madness in their hearts while they live, and afterward they join the dead. ⁴Anyone who is among the living has hope — even a live dog is better off than a dead lion!**

⁵For the living know that they will die,
　　but the dead know nothing;
　they have no further reward,
　　and even the memory of them is forgotten.
⁶Their love, their hate
　　and their jealousy have long since vanished;
　never again will they have a part
　　in anything that happens under the sun.

Everyone under the sun meets the same end. Viewing life and death from a purely human perspective, it's only natural to conclude that it doesn't matter how you live. Death is such a stark reality that it can overpower people's innate sense of eternity, as well as their natural knowledge of God and the voice of conscience.

We're all going to die! We observe that good people die along with the wicked. As we do so, we can sense the evil within our own hearts. "Out of men's hearts," declared Jesus, "come evil thoughts, sexual immorality, theft, murder, adultery, greed, malice, deceit, lewdness, envy, slander, arrogance and folly" (Mark 7:21,22). No matter what you do you'll die anyway, so why not follow every desire of your heart?

Not only are men's hearts "full of evil," but, Solomon continues, there is also "madness in their hearts." One commentator describes this madness as "unbridled and unprincipled conduct, which results from the conviction that life is meaningless and that there is no moral law operating in the world."[12] A modern song says it more bluntly, as it screams to a new generation, "Let's go crazy!" Poet Dylan Thomas expressed the relation between madness and death with his well-known lines,

　Do not go gentle into the good night,
　Old age should burn and rave at close of day;
　Rage, rage against the dying of the light.

Within each human heart rage sin and madness, storming to get out before life's brief flame is extinguished. For the Christian this means there is a war within his heart. St. Paul put it this way: "I see another law at work in the members of my body, waging war against the law of my mind" (Romans 7:23). Through his word, God has called us to faith. Now he calls upon us as knights of faith to wage a daily battle against the dragons of sin and madness within.

There are many who have given up this fight, or who never even entered it in the first place. For such people, the lusts of the heart have conquered. Their lives are controlled by the sin and madness within. Thus in *The Sun Also Rises* Hemingway depicted young, but world-weary, heroes living only for the day's brief pleasures.

In the end both Christian and unbeliever "join the dead." For the child of God it marks the end of the torment within. For the unbeliever it is only the beginning.

The Teacher's words "Anyone who is among the living has hope" remind us of another ancient expression, "Where there's life there's hope." Solomon's words apply to the wicked and to the godly. For the worldly person death brings an end to all his hopes and dreams. It also brings an end to his time of grace and any hope of salvation. There is a way in which death marks the end of some of our hopes. For example, only while we remain on earth can we hope to testify to others. Remember Paul's words, "I desire to depart and be with Christ, which is better by far; but it is more necessary for you that I remain in the body" (Philippians 1:23,24).

In saying that "a live dog is better off than a dead lion," Solomon might well be quoting a common cliche of his day. He uses the cliche to back up his statement about the hope of the living. We do the same kind of thing when we talk. We make a point and then finish it off with, "You know what they always say. . . . "

At any rate, Solomon's picture sticks in our minds. The typical dog in the orient was a scavenger. To call someone a dog was a real insult. For instance, when he was accused of wrongdoing, Abner felt insulted and blurted out, "Am I a dog's head?" (2 Samuel 3:8) Revelation 22:15 describes the damned as "the dogs." As much as dogs are enjoyed and pampered in our day, the canine species still has not reached complete respectability. To call someone a "dirty dog" or just plain "dog" is hardly a compliment. The lion on the other hand has always been respected as the savage but majestic king of the beasts. Proverbs 30:30 describes the lion as "mighty among beasts, who retreats before nothing." Yet even a little scavenger dog roaming the streets is better off than a dead lion, because he still has life.

Back in Ecclesiastes 4:2 Solomon had declared that "the dead . . . are happier than the living." Now he speaks of certain advantages the living have over the dead. He is not contradicting himself, but simply viewing the subject from a different angle.

One advantage the living have is that they still play an active role under the sun. They are conscious of things, including the fact that "they will die." But "the dead know nothing." This can apply only to life under the sun. Certainly the dead are conscious of God's judgment; but they do not know what happens on earth. Isaiah 63:16 substantiates this. Speaking of the long-dead patriarchs, Abraham and Israel, it says, "Abraham does not know us or Israel acknowledge us."

Moreover, the dead are no longer around to enjoy any "further reward" on earth, and as time goes by "even the memory of them is forgotten."

95

When people leave this world their emotions — "their love, their hate and their jealousy" — go with them. Those once driving emotions vanish from the scene.

The Teacher sums up this section on death with the words, "Never again will they have a part in anything that happens under the sun." Those who hope for "another time around" through some sort of reincarnation are whistling in the dark. "Man is destined to die once, and after that to face judgment" (Hebrews 9:27). Once you leave this earth, it's final. You'll never come back. Never.

> **⁷Go, eat your food with gladness,**
> **and drink your wine with a joyful heart,**
> **for it is now that God favors what you do.**
> **⁸Always be clothed in white,**
> **and always anoint your head with oil.**
>
> **⁹Enjoy life with your wife, whom you love, all the days of this meaningless life that God has given you under the sun — all your meaningless days. For this is your lot in life and in your toilsome labor under the sun. ¹⁰Whatever your hand finds to do, do it with all your might, for in the grave, where you are going, there is neither working nor planning nor knowledge nor wisdom.**

Death is certain. Life is short. Once you've gone, you'll never return to live on this earth. Why, then, waste time fretting over things you can't control? "Enjoy life," urges the Teacher. You can enjoy life without abandoning yourself to sin and madness.

Eat, drink, and be merry! — not with the attitude of the Epicureans, not because life is meaningless and nothing else matters, but realizing that food and wine and clothes and human love are all gifts from the hand of God. God is favoring you with these gifts *now*, so why foolishly wait until some future date?

St. Paul told his young co-worker Timothy, "Stop drinking only water, and use a little wine because of your stomach and your frequent illnesses" (1 Timothy 5:23). Like other food and drink, wine is good, even medicinal, if not used in excess. Take pleasure in the moderate use of God's good gifts!

From wine Solomon moves to the topic of clothing. The ancient Jews dressed up for festive occasions in white clothing and anointed their heads with oil. Olive oil and white clothes were associated with happiness. The Bible uses these customs to symbolize the spiritual joy of God's people. Isaiah foretells how the Savior will "bestow on" his people "the oil of gladness" (Isaiah 61:3). St. John depicts the saints in heaven as those who "have washed their robes and made them white" (Revelation 7:14).

For those who are married, Solomon mentions another blessing. "Enjoy life with your wife, whom you love." One of life's greatest blessings is a loving husband or wife. The Teacher is not advocating that a person go out and find a different partner if he or she doesn't like the present one. Solomon is tying love and marriage together, as God intends. If we are married we must constantly work at making it a loving relationship. Simply recognizing the fact that your partner is a gift from God does much to keep your married love alive.

Marriage is a temporary blessing. "At the resurrection people will neither marry nor be given in marriage" (Matthew 22:30). So instead of spending years in discontent and bitterness, married people should enjoy their companionship during their short "meaningless" life on earth. A good wife is a priceless help "in your toilsome labor under the sun."

Solomon's thoughts on enjoying life find a striking parallel in some ancient literature from Babylon. *The Gilgamesh Epic*, an ancient flood story dating back to about 2000 B.C., contains these words of advice to the hero Gilgamesh:

Thou, O Gilgamesh, let thy belly be full;
Day and night be thou merry;
Make every day a day of rejoicing.
Day and night do thou dance and play.
Let thy raiment be clean;
Thy head be washed, and thy self be bathed in water.
Cherish the little one holding thy hand,
And let thy wife rejoice in thy bosom.
This is the lot of mankind.[13]

These words help demonstrate that throughout the centuries non-Christians have also seen the value of enjoying life. But only the Bible puts that enjoyment into proper spiritual perspective. Enjoyment must be balanced with our obligations to serve God and our fellow man.

All life's pleasures must also be balanced with the reality of work. The Teacher tells us there is only one way to approach work, namely, "with all your might." Whatever work you have found, do your best at it. If you're a student, study hard. If you are a parent, learn from God's Word what is best for your children, and then do it. Do you work in a factory or an office, a store or a school? Are you a salesman, a homemaker, a baker, a preacher, a truck driver, a police officer, a soldier, a lawyer, a nurse . . . ? Do not spend your time complaining about your job or wishing you had someone else's talents. Just do the work God has placed in front of you. And do the best *you* can with it.

In the book of Proverbs Solomon frequently speaks out against laziness. "How long will you lie there, you sluggard?" asks Solomon. "When will you get up from your sleep?" (Proverbs 6:9) In Ecclesiastes the Teacher explains why it's important to work to capacity. You can't go back and do it over again. If you didn't study in school, if you wasted your talents, if you've neglected your children, if you have hurt others through you negligence — you may not get a chance to make amends or to do the job over the right way. Finally, in the grave, all opportunity will have been lost.

The word translated "grave" is the Hebrew term *sheol.* You may have come across some commentaries or versions of the Bible that leave it untranslated. If refers to the entire realm of the dead. Depending on the context in which it occurs, *sheol* has a wide range of specific meanings: the state of death, the grave, sometimes even hell. Whatever its specific designation, once you have entered *sheol* you can no longer return to life on earth.

When it comes to working for our Savior, the urgency is all the greater. "As long as it is day, we must do the work of him who sent me," says Jesus. "Night is coming, when no one can work" (John 9:4). Whatever you can do for God, "do it with all your might."

> [11]I have seen something else under the sun:
> The race is not to the swift
> or the battle to the strong,
> nor does food come to the wise
> or wealth to the brilliant
> or favor to the learned;
> but time and chance happen to them all.
> [12]Moreover, no man knows when his hour will come:
> As fish are caught in a cruel net,
> or birds are taken in a snare,
> so men are trapped by evil times
> that fall unexpectedly upon them.

No matter how ably and hard we work, we dare not boast about the outcome. That is in God's hands, and we must humbly leave it there.

Solomon gives a number of examples to demonstrate that this truth applies to every area of life. Sometimes the fastest runner falls down and loses the race, as has happened in

Olympic games. Sometimes a stronger army loses to a weaker one, as when the Midianite armies, who were as "thick as locusts," were defeated by Gideon and his 300 men (Judges 7). A truly wise man might live in poverty, while some foolish person wins a fortune in a lottery or signs a multi-million dollar contract to play baseball. A brilliant artist may die penniless, never to be "discovered" until he's gone. A skilled and knowledgeable worker may get nothing but contempt instead of praise for his efforts.

"But time and chance happen to them all." That is, God decides their lot. Therefore we should learn to depend on God and not on human factors. As the Psalmist states,

No king is saved by the size of his army;
no warrior escapes by his great strength.
A horse is a vain hope for deliverance;
despite all its great strength it cannot save.
But the eyes of the Lord are on those who fear him,
on those whose hope is in his unfailing love,
to deliver them from death
and keep them alive in famine. (Psalm 33:16-19)

Solomon goes on to state that the hour of death comes quickly and unexpectedly for many. Did you ever think of how it must feel to be a fish, swimming along and suddenly find yourself caught in a net? Or a bird, drawn into a snare by some bait or decoy? In a moment it's all over.

It is not only death that can spring on us like a trap. "Evil times . . . fall unexpectedly." Just when people are out celebrating, thinking that they've got it made, tragedy strikes: an accident, a sudden illness, a loss in the family, financial ruin, national disaster. This is another reason for us to live life one day at a time, trusting in God.

Wisdom Better Than Folly

13I also saw under the sun this example of wisdom that greatly impressed me: 14There was once a small city with only a few

people in it. And a powerful king came against it, surrounded it and built huge siegeworks against it. [15]Now there lived in that city a man poor but wise, and he saved the city by his wisdom. But nobody remembered that poor man. [16]So I said, "Wisdom is better than strength." But the poor man's wisdom is despised, and his words are no longer heeded.

> [17]The quiet words of the wise are more to be heeded
> than the shouts of a ruler of fools.
> [18]Wisdom is better than weapons of war,
> but one sinner destroys much good.

Solomon does not say who this poor but wise man was. Most likely the history had been lost, as the king indicates with the remark, "But nobody remembered that poor man."

Nor does King Solomon tell us how the wise man "saved the city by his wisdom." Did he personally talk the enemy king out of fighting? Did he devise some ingenious strategy to defeat the powerful king? Solomon withholds the information because that, too, is beside the point. His point is simply this: as valuable as wisdom can be and for all the good it can do for others, there is no guarantee that a good and wise person will be rewarded under the sun.

When the people in the small city were desperate they listened to the poor wise man. Once the city was safe "nobody remembered that poor man." Maybe as soon as the danger had passed people attributed their deliverance to luck. Or perhaps some boastful official took all the credit for himself.

One commentator suggests that the poor man was despised "because he does not possess an imposing splendid outward appearance, in accordance with which the crowd estimates the value of a man's words."[14] It can easily happen in politics today. The man who looks better on TV wins an election. It can also happen in the church. People flock to hear the preacher who cuts an imposing figure and has a magnificent voice or a clever way with words, mistaking such things for depth of message.

Because of these sad realities, Solomon adds this proverb: "The quiet words of the wise are more to be heeded than the shouts of a ruler of fools." Learn to listen beyond the loud impressive voice. Sometimes the most priceless wisdom is concealed in the plainest wrappings. Often the voice of God himself comes not with the roaring of the wind or the shaking of an earthquake or the raging of a fire, but with "a gentle whisper" (1 Kings 19:11,12).

The king closes this section with another proverb. "Wisdom is better than weapons of war, but one sinner destroys much good." It takes years to build a beautiful cathedral, but one careless act can reduce it to ashes. One thoughtless evil deed can undo much good.

Wisdom seems to be a very fragile gift. It is easily forgotten. It often goes unrewarded. And it is quickly undone. Still, says wise King Solomon, for all its delicacy, "wisdom is better than weapons of war." Wisdom builds up and saves life, rather than destroying it.

10 As dead flies give perfume a bad smell,
so little folly outweighs wisdom and honor.
²The heart of the wise inclines to the right,
but the heart of the fool to the left.
³Even as he walks along the road,
the fool lacks sense
and shows everyone how stupid he is.

Ecclesiastes 10 is like a slice from the book of Proverbs. The Teacher-king raps out one short proverb or wise-saying after another. Often there is little or no transition as Solomon jumps from one thought to the next. Yet there is a consistent theme running through the chapter: wisdom is better than folly. Solomon backs up this theme with many examples from life. He offers us wisdom to apply to our lives — godly wisdom for life under the sun.

"Dead flies" are literally "flies of death." The expression might mean flies that are dead or flies that are deadly, poisonous. In either case, when these flies get stuck in oily perfume, they give it a bad odor. The Hebrew word for fly is worth an interesting little digression. The word is *zebub* (you can almost hear the buzzing). Combining it with the word *baal* or *beel* (meaning lord, master), we have Beelzebub, the lord of the flies who bring disease and death. This is one of the names we have come to apply to Satan, "the prince of demons" (Matthew 12:24). The devil is the lord of the filthy, disease-bringing kingdom of the evil demons.

Just as one little fly can make a whole bottle of perfume stink, "so a little folly outweighs wisdom and honor." It takes only one foolish little mistake or one thoughtless slip of the tongue from a high official such as a president and, before you know it, every newspaper and newscast is carrying it. It could mean the end of an excellent career. It might even decide the course of history. Whether we are public figures or not, the words apply to all of us. Have you ever committed "a little folly" which you've spent years trying to live down? Most of us can speak from experience here.

Comparing the wise man and the fool, Solomon uses the directions "right" and "left." Right frequently symbolizes good and left bad, as when Jesus says he "will put the sheep on his right and the goats on his left" on Judgment Day (Matthew 25:33). Solomon is comparing godly wisdom with the lack thereof. The wise man trusts in God. The fool, on the other hand, disregards God and his word. In the end such a person will end up on the left. He will be damned.

Solomon pictures the fool walking "along the road." This refers to when he is out in public in contrast to being at home. Deuteronomy 6:7 puts the two side by side; there we are told to be attentive to God's commandments no matter where we are. "Talk about them when you sit at home and when you walk along the road." The fool, however, ignores God's word both in public and private.

Solomon is not necessarily depicting some kind of clown when he says the fool "shows everyone how stupid he is." The fool may be clever and disguise his talk with a cloak of pseudo-wisdom. And there may just be enough people out there who are themselves fools, and who look upon his stupidity as the highest wisdom!

> ⁴If a ruler's anger rises against you,
>   do not leave your post;
>   calmness can lay great errors to rest.
> ⁵There is an evil I have seen under the sun,
>   the sort of error that arises from a ruler:
> ⁶Fools are put in many high positions,
>   while the rich occupy the low ones.
> ⁷I have seen slaves on horseback,
>   while princes go on foot like slaves.

Instead of being recognized for what they are, fools often rise to important positions under the sun. Solomon now adds a few proverbs on that subject.

First he urges us not to give in to the unjust anger of others, even if they are people in authority. If you know what you have done is right and in keeping with God's word, stick to it. Maybe your boss is angry with you because you were honest or didn't take advantage of some customer. Don't go along with him. And don't become angry and quit. Be calm. The "ruler" may even come to his senses and thank you for it in the end. Think of how the Prophet Nathan calmly reproved King David for his sins of adultery and murder (2 Samuel 12:1-13). Had Nathan not spoken so boldly to the king, David might never have repented of his sins.

The fact is, Solomon continues, rulers can be as foolish and in need of correction as anyone. This is another of life's evils. Sad to say, the wrong people are often in the wrong places under the sun. Fools are "in many high positions" while "the rich occupy the low ones." In this context "rich" must mean someone who is rich in wisdom and knowledge. Similarly "slaves on horseback, while princes go on foot" is a way of saying things are mixed up. They aren't what they should be.

This upside-down world produces many an "error." On the spur of the moment King Herod makes a half-drunken promise to a dancing girl (Mark 16:14-29). This error results in the beheading of John the Baptist, whom Jesus had honored as the greatest individual of the entire Old Testament era (Matthew 11:11). Our century has witnessed the whole world plunged into war, largely because of one man's lust for power.

Luther comments, "So it is that the fool is in charge everywhere, prevailing in the senate, in the court of rulers, etc. The world is foolish, and it is ruled by fools and by foolish opinions."

It is good for us to keep these truths in mind. They prevent us from being overawed by the words of the high and mighty. They also lead us to the Scriptures, the only source of real wisdom.

⁸Whoever digs a pit may fall into it;
whoever breaks through a wall may be bitten by a snake.
⁹Whoever quarries stones may be injured by them;
whoever splits logs may be endangered by them.
¹⁰If the ax is dull
and its edge unsharpened,
more strength is needed
but skill will bring success.
¹¹If a snake bites before it is charmed,
there is no profit for the charmer.

In these four verses Solomon draws on occupations and experiences of his day to present some timeless truths.

In verse 8 he seems to show that evil intentions can recoil on those who are out to harm others. Psalm 57:6 also uses the imagery of digging a pit to trap someone. "They dug a pit in my path — but they have fallen into it themselves." The other pictures, that of breaking through a wall, possibly refers to a person trying to break into someone else's field or house. The land of Israel has always been very stoney. Farmers still use the stones from their fields to build dividing walls or hillside terraces. In breaking through such loosely constructed walls, a person might disturb a snake from some crevice. Solomon's point — in seeking to harm others many people end up harming only themselves.

While the activities mentioned in verse 8 might well be ill-intended, those described in verse 9 are not. Nevertheless, they can still harm the person involved. The work of quarrying stones was big business in Solomon's day. When he built the temple "Solomon had seventy thousand carriers and eighty thousand stone cutters in the hills, as well as thirty-three hundred foremen who supervised the project and directed the workmen. At the king's command they removed from the quarry large blocks of quality stone" (1 Kings 5:15-17). No doubt it could be dangerous work removing those large blocks. The other work that the Teacher mentions in verse 9, log splitting, was also involved in constructing the temple. "The craftsmen of Solomon . . . cut and prepared the timber and stone for the building of the temple" (1 Kings 5:18). The Bible mentions one of the dangers connected with such work. "A man may go into the forest with his neighbor to cut wood, and as he swings his ax to fell a tree, the head may fly off and hit his neighbor and kill him" (Deuteronomy 19:5).

106

Solomon is saying that there is danger in honest labor as well as in dishonest work. Consequently, we should pray for God's guidance and help and see to it that our work is God-pleasing.

The king's words about an ax are not hard to understand. If the ax is dull, the workman needs more strength than if he's working with a sharp ax. "But skill will bring success." That is, you'll save a lot of effort if you have someone around who is skillful enough to sharpen the ax! In a way, we are all dulled, imperfect axes because of sin. When God uses our services he needs both strength and skill to carry out the work. Parents, too, need skill to sharpen their children for useful lives in God's kingdom.

The verse about the snake charmer has a double meaning. Of course, a snake charmer is going to lose business if his snake bites someone before it rises for the charmer. Interestingly, the words translated "charmer" literally mean "a master of the tongue." Understood in this way, Solomon is also saying, "Watch that tongue of yours. Don't speak before you think." David expressed a similar thought. "Rescue me, O Lord, from evil men; . . . they make their tongues as sharp as a serpent's; the poison of vipers is on their lips" (Psalm 140:1,3). We should learn to charm our tongues *before* they bite. James says it very strongly. "If anyone considers himself religious and yet does not keep a tight rein on his tongue, he decieves himself and his religion is worthless" (James 1:26).

> [12]Words from a wise man's mouth are gracious,
>   but a fool is consumed by his own lips.
> [13]At the beginning his words are folly;
>   at the end they are wicked madness —
> [14]   and the fool multiplies words.
>   No one knows what is coming —
>   who can tell him what will happen after him?

> **¹⁵A fool's work wearies him;**
> **he does not know the way to town.**

We live in an age which has come to disregard the importance of words. "Actions speak louder than words" is an
oft-repeated cliche. Moreover, many today view language
merely as a means to stir up emotions, rather than a means
to convey objective truth. In advertising and popular music
— and also in politics and religion — *what* is said often takes
a back seat to *how* it is said.

The Bible frequently stresses that words (along with actions and thoughts) are important. It is through human
words that the almighty God has revealed himself to us. We,
in turn, are to be careful with our speech. Earlier Solomon
showed that what we say to God is not to be taken lightly.
"Do not be quick with your mouth . . . to utter anything
before God" (5:2). Now he emphasizes that we should also
be concerned about our speech to others. Our words and the
manner in which we say them are important.

"Words from a wise man's mouth are gracious." What
does it mean to have "gracious" words? It means to answer
others "with gentleness and respect" (1 Peter 3:16), to keep
"filthy language from your lips" (Colossians 3:8) and "to
speak the truth in love" (Ephesians 4:15).

The Teacher contrasts the wise man's gracious speech
with the fool's words. The proverb, "A fool is consumed by
his own lips," is similar to the present-day expression, "He
puts his foot in his mouth." In his speech the fool goes from
bad to worse — from "folly" to "wicked madness." He
"multiplies words." Perhaps he starts with a "little white lie,"
then turns to lengthy cover-ups. Peter's denial of Christ is a
classic example of this (Matthew 26:69-75). When a servant
girl asserted he was with Christ, Peter replied, "I don't know
what you're talking about." When approached a second

time, "he denied it again, with an oath: 'I don't know the man!' " When the people standing around still kept after Peter, "he began to call down curses on himself and he swore to them, 'I don't know the man!' "

Have you ever found yourself "multiplying words" to try to get out of an awkward situation? or simply to assert your presence? Saying too much is not wise, for it can lead us to say things we shouldn't. "When words are many, sin is not absent, but he who holds his tongue is wise" (Proverbs 10:19).

The fool has a lot to say on many different subjects, including the future, about which he knows nothing. James, who seems to draw heavily from Ecclesiastes, offers this advice in a passage already referred to:

> Now listen, you who say, "Today or tomorrow we will go to this or that city, spend a year there, carry on business and make money." Why, you do not even know what will happen tomorrow. What is your life? You are a mist that appears for a little while and then vanishes. Instead, you ought to say, "If it is the Lord's will, we will live and do this or that." As it is, you boast and brag. All such boasting is evil. (James 4:13-16)

The fool makes his plans, talks on and on, and endlessly carries on his labors, even to the point of exhaustion. He may have very definite ambitions and plans. In reality all his work is meaningless, because his endeavors are without God. So the fool aimlessly wanders through life. In this sense, "he does not know the way to town."

> **[16]Woe to you, O land whose king was a servant
>   and whose princes feast in the morning.
> [17]Blessed are you, O land whose king is of noble birth
>   and whose princes eat at a proper time —
>   for strength and not for drunkenness.**

> ¹⁸If a man is lazy, the rafters sag;
> if his hands are idle, the house leaks.
> ¹⁹A feast is made for laughter,
> and wine makes life merry,
> but money is the answer for everything.
> ²⁰Do not revile the king even in your thoughts,
> or curse the rich in your bedroom,
> because a bird of the air may carry your words,
> and a bird on the wing may report what you say.

What a tragedy when foolish people come to power and rule an entire nation! The word for "servant" here literally means "child." Regardless of his numerical age, he is immature and more interested in enjoying life and the privileges of power than in guiding the people and seeking their welfare. Little did King Solomon know that after his death his own son Rehoboam would "reject the advice the elders gave him and consult the young men who had grown up with him" (1 Kings 12:8). So Solomon's words proved prophetic, although he did not mean them that way.

A country can consider itself "blessed" when its king or leader "is of noble birth." King Solomon's point is not that the leader must come from high society or the nobility, but with his own noble traits. This kind of ruler keeps his balance. He and his advisors are effective and good at what we might call time-management. They work during the day. When they break for eating, they dine "for strength and not for drunkenness." These words remind us of a passage from Proverbs: "It is not for kings . . . to drink wine, not for rulers to crave beer, lest they drink and forget what the law decrees, and deprive all the oppressed of their rights" (Proverbs 31:4,5).

The Teacher's frequent emphasis on good leadership impresses on us how grateful we should be for capable leaders in our government. We can be thankful for wise leaders in the past, men like Andrew Jackson, who spoke of the Bible as "the rock on which our republic stands." We should pray for such leaders today.

As is his custom, Solomon immediately contrasts the good with the bad. The opposite of a good, industrious leader is the lazy man. If the lazy person is a homeowner he lets the roof sag and leak. If the lazy man is a leader in the government or the church, that house soon starts to sag and leak. When leadership is sluggish, corruption and immorality can begin to creep into an organization.

Indeed, there is a time for feasting, laughter, wine and merriment. The wise person will know when that time is and not let it interfere with his duties in life. Rather than overindulging in these pleasures, he will recognize them as God's gifts for needed times of recreation and relaxation.

The lazy and self-indulgent whom Solomon has been describing do not have this perspective. For them life holds nothing more than the pursuit of pleasure. It appears that Solomon inserted the last line of verse 19 as a further illustration of their attitude — "money is the answer for everything." In earlier chapters the Teacher had stressed that money is *not* the answer. In and of themselves, riches are meaningless (5:8-6:12). How sad, then, when people — especially people of influence — can't see beyond their own greed.

Even if we happen to live under this kind of ruler or work for this sort of boss, we still owe him respect because of his position. We should take his words and actions in the kindest possible way and not belittle him or speak evil of him. This proper attitude begins in our hearts, with our thoughts. If our hearts are full of bitterness and resentment, sooner or later it will come out in an ill-advised utterance. "For out of the overflow of the heart," says Jesus, "the mouth speaks"

111

(Matthew 12:34). It happens often enough that servants curse their masters (7:21,22), employees curse their bosses and citizens curse their officials. And before you know it, a little bird has carried your words back to where you don't want them to go. You may end up losing your job or, if you live under an oppressive government, your life.

It's not that the Bible is advising us to be cowards and play it safe. If there are wrongs that need correcting, we should confront the wrongdoer directly. Jesus instructs us, "If your brother sins against you, go and show him his fault between the two of you" (Matthew 18:15). This is the correct, loving approach. It is not right to let the word leak back second- or third-hand.

Bread Upon the Waters

11 Cast your bread upon the waters,
    for after many days you will find it again.
    [2]Give portions to seven, yes to eight,
        for you do not know what disaster may come
        upon the land

Solomon is nearing the end of his presentation. With a series of colorful proverbs he now calls on us to work diligently and then to leave the results to God.

First of all, we are to trust God to bless the good we do for others. To convey this thought Solomon tells us to "cast [the Hebrew word can also mean "send"] bread upon the waters." He is probably alluding to merchant ships sent out with bread, that is, goods for trade. King Solomon himself "had a fleet of trading ships. . . . Once every three years it returned carrying gold, silver and ivory, and apes and baboons" (1 Kings 10:22). From the Red Sea port of Ezion Geber (1 Kings 9:26) his ships sailed to Arabia and possibly on to faraway India.

Just as it took faith that the fleet would eventually return with its cargo, so we need faith that the good we send out into the world will finally return with a cargo of blessings. Just as the wind and waves carried the fleet out of sight and out of mind, we should do good and forget about it. Then, perhaps years later, when we least expect it, the good comes back.

Many pastors have had the experience of a former member unexpectedly stopping in to visit and reminding them of some kind deed from years ago. It's the type of experience every Christian can have. Most likely we will not get much return in this life; Ecclesiastes had made it clear enough that life isn't like that. But sooner or later deeds of love done from a God-given faith will have their reward. Jesus points out that the greatest and most selfless works of love may not receive any return in this life. Yet, like the merchant ships, they will finally come back filled with blessings.

> When you give a luncheon or dinner, do not invite your friends, your brothers or relatives, or your rich neighbors; if you do, they may invite you back and so you will be repaid. But when you give a banquet, invite the poor, the crippled, the lame, the blind, and you will be blessed. Although they cannot repay you, you will be repaid at the resurrection of the righteous. (Luke 14:12-14)

In telling us to "give portions to seven, yes to eight," the Teacher urges us to be generous. The theme of generosity is found throughout Scripture. For example, St. Paul cautions, "Remember this: Whoever sows sparingly will also reap sparingly, and whoever sows generously will also reap generously. . . . God loves a cheerful giver" (2 Corinthians 9:6,7).

We do not know "what disaster may come upon the land." God could send famines, crop failures, economic depressions, and countless other troubles. Whenever disaster strikes we want to do what we can to help those in need. Perhaps someday when we ourselves are in need, our generosity will be repaid. Solomon had previously discussed the tragedy of hoarding goods, only to have them fall into the hands of a person who neither needs them nor uses them properly (2:18-21). Now he offers an alternative to such miserliness — giving to the needy.

The expression "to seven, yes to eight" describes a sort of generosity that isn't concerned about exact numbers. We are not to help others simply to build up a record of ourselves. More important than keeping track of how many people we've helped is that our giving be motivated by love.

> ³If clouds are full of water,
>   they pour rain upon the earth.
> Whether a tree falls to the south or to the north,
>   in the place where it falls, there will it lie.
> ⁴Whoever watches the wind will not plant;
>   whoever looks at the clouds will not reap.
> ⁵As you do not know the path of the wind,
>   or how the body is formed in a mother's womb,
> so you cannot understand the work of God,
>   the Maker of all things.
> ⁶Sow your seed in the morning,
>   and at evening let not your hands be idle,
> for you do not know which will succeed,
>   whether this or that,
>   or whether both will do equally well.

What will be will be. If it's going to rain, it will rain. If a tree falls this way or that, wherever it falls "there will it lie." Consequently, we can go about our lives and not worry about what may or may not happen.

Some people are constantly checking the wind and clouds for just "the right time" to begin their ventures. Such undue caution is not the mark of bold faith in God's control of the future. "Let us not become weary in doing good," says Paul, "for at the proper time we will reap a harvest if we do not give up" (Galatians 6:10). In every aspect of life, but especially in doing the Lord's work, confident and persistent action is the proper approach.

Often things turn out quite differently from the way we could ever have foreseen it. We can't see the wind blowing, nor can we watch an infant develop within its mother's womb. That's how it is with God's ways. This is important to remember when doing mission work or evangelism. Jesus combines both the pictures of the wind and the baby when he describes God's way of bringing people to faith: "The wind blows wherever it pleases. You hear its sound but you cannot tell where it comes from or where it is going. So it is with everyone born of the Spirit" (John 3:8). A Christian may share his faith with an unbeliever and meet with nothing but rejection and apparent failure. Meanwhile the Spirit of God is invisibly at work through the word planted in the unbeliever. Perhaps after many years that person is born into God's family of faith.

The Teacher's final illustration in this section — that of sowing seeds — lends itself to similar applications. In whatever we attempt we should do our best and leave the results to God. Rather than staking everything on one venture, Solomon advises us to make use of numerous opportunities. "For you do not know which will succeed. . . . " Again, the application is especially fitting in the spiritual realm. Whenever and however possible, we should plant the seeds of God's word. Only God knows where and when results will come from the effort.

Throughout the Bible God compares nature — the rain, wind, planting, growth — with spiritual realities — the planting of God's word, spiritual growth, the Christian life.

Jesus' parables are filled with these comparisons. His well-known parable of the sower and the seeds (Matthew 13:1-23) is reminiscent of King Solomon's words about the seed. Such simple, down-to-earth illustrations call us to look more closely at God's wonderful creation. It has a lot to teach us.

Remember Your Creator While Young

> [7]Light is sweet,
>   and it pleases the eyes to see the sun.
> [8]However many years a man may live,
>   let him enjoy them all.
> But let him remember the days of darkness,
>   for they will be many.
> Everything to come is meaningless.
> [9]Be happy, young man, while you are young,
>   and let your heart give you joy in the days
>   of your youth.
> Follow the ways of your heart
>   and whatever your eyes see,
> but know that for all these things
>   God will bring you to judgment.
> [10]So then, banish anxiety from your heart
>   and cast off the troubles of your body,
>   for youth and vigor are meaningless.

Work hard. Leave the results to God. And then enjoy life. Approached in this way, life under the sun can be sweet. Enjoy the days of sunshine and happiness. Try to find enjoyment in life as long as you live.

Whatever joy we find, of course, is tempered by "the days of darkness," which "will be many." When Solomon speaks in this way, he is not an embittered old man. He is simply telling it like it is. He is expressing the realism which runs through the entire Bible. Five centuries before Solomon's

116

time, Moses said in a similar vein, "The length of our days is seventy years — or eighty, if we have the strength; yet their span is but trouble and sorrow, for they quickly pass, and we fly away" (Psalm 90:10). Solomon's statement, "Everything to come is meaningless," underscores the troubled and fleeting nature of life on earth.

The old king now directs his thoughts to young people. "Be happy, young man, while you are young, and let your heart give you joy. . . . " Generally youth is a time of energy, freshness, love for life and a sense of adventure. Like spring flowers, youthful joys all too often wither beneath the weaknesses and problems of aging. So Solomon urges, "Be happy . . . let your heart give you joy. . . . Follow the ways of your heart and whatever your eyes see."

Some commentators see in this passage a contradiction of God's words given through Moses in Numbers 15:39: " . . . remember all the commands of the Lord, that you may obey them and not prostitute yourselves by going after the lusts of your own hearts and eyes." As we consider the context of Solomon's words, however, it's clear he is not telling young people to follow the lusts and evil desires of their eyes and hearts. Solomon is talking about God-pleasing pursuits of youth — things like pursuing an education, traveling, going out with friends, getting married, laughing, playing games and just having a good time.

The king immediately rules out youthful lusts such as drunkenness, sexual promiscuity, hatred, jealously and laziness, when he adds, "But know that for all these things God will bring you to judgment." Enjoyment has its limitations. It is circumscribed by God's commands. Many a youth has sown wild oats, only to live with the consequences for a lifetime. And beyond this life there is the judgment to come.

Luther's thoughts on this passage are worth sharing at length. Luther said,

Above all, young people should avoid sadness and loneliness. Joy is as necessary for youth as food and drink, for the body is invigorated by a happy spirit. Education should not begin with the body but with the spirit, so that this is not overlooked; for when the spirit has been properly instructed, it is easy to govern the body. Therefore one must be indulgent with youth, and must let them be happy and do everything with a happy spirit. Yet one must see to it that they are not corrupted by the desires of the flesh. For carousals, drinking-bouts, and love affairs are not the happiness of the heart of which he is speaking here, for they instead make the spirit sad.

Many young people think that religion is going to put a damper on their fun. In a sense it will. Young people who try to live their faith are going to have to say no to much of what is considered fun by their peers. But Solomon looks at it another way. An awareness of God's judgment helps you "banish anxiety from your heart and cast off the troubles of your body." How? The person who tries to live according to God's Word enjoys freedoms and pleasures which can never be found in sinful indulgence. He has peace of conscience and peace with God. His mind is not assailed by an accusing conscience, nor his body weighed down with worries that his evil deeds will catch up with him.

Good advice, isn't it? Savor the bright days of youth, "for youth and vigor are meaningless." The Hebrew word translated "vigor" is most likely related to the word denoting "blackness of hair." It stands in contrast to old age when the hair turns white or is lost. The time of youth is short. The vigor of youth is as fleeting as a vapor.

12   **Remember your Creator
in the days of your youth,**

before the days of trouble come
and the years approach when you will say,
"I find no pleasure in them" —
[2]before the sun and the light
and the moon and the stars grow dark,
and the clouds return after the rain;
[3]when the keepers of the house tremble,
and the strong men stoop,
when the grinders cease because they are few,
and those looking through the windows grow dim;
[4]when the doors to the street are closed
and the sound of grinding fades;
when men rise up at the sound of birds,
but all their songs grow faint;
[5]when men are afraid of heights
and of dangers in the streets;
when the almond tree blossoms
and the grasshopper drags himself along
and desire no longer is stirred.
Then man goes to his eternal home
and mourners go about the streets.

Since this section continues the thought of the previous chapter, the division between chapters 11 and 12 might have been made at a better place. Here Solomon moves from the subject of youth to old age and death. These verses constitute one of the most moving and beautiful portions of Ecclesiastes, indeed in all of literature.

When Solomon says, "Remember your Creator," he means more than just, "Think about God." Rather, he uses the word remember as the Prophet Malachi does when he declares, "Remember the law" (Malachi 4:4). God is not satisfied that we simply remember him as we might some fact of history or bit of trivia. To remember him means to keep him and his word constantly in mind and heart, to trust in him and live each new day with him and for him. It means to be thankful for all his gifts and promises and to call on him in time of need.

Young people shouldn't get the idea that they can forget about God until they are older. That day may never come. People who have lived their lives without God do not easily find him at the eleventh hour. For every thief on the cross who is saved at the end of his life (Luke 23:39-43), there are countless others who pass through death's dark door in the same way they lived their lives — unprepared to meet their Maker. *Now* is the time for God. Now is the time for Bible study, prayer and church attendance. Then, as life's troubles mount, we can meet them with God at our side.

Of this we can be sure: "the days of trouble" will come. Should we live long enough, the years will come when we will say, "I find no pleasure in them." Having asserted this, Solomon proceeds to paint a very poetic picture of the arrival of old age. He depicts a village scene on an overcast, cloudy day. Each aspect of the picture represents a feature of old age.

First Solomon mentions that the sun, moon and stars "grow dark." This points to the sadness of growing old. Friends and loved ones die. Loneliness and sickness set in. The days of productivity are past. Many an old person longs for the day he or she will leave the dark valley of life on earth.

"The clouds return after the rain." When we are young sunshine follows the rain. But as life's sicknesses, heartaches and problems pile up, recovery doesn't come so quickly. An old person often gets through one sickness or trouble only to have another follow on its heels. Hengstenberg correctly notes that this piling up of troubles serves two purposes — one for believers, the other for unbelievers. "The power to suffer is exhausted in old age; the heart is already broken:

that is however not the only consideration here. God's will is to melt down his own people completely before the end of life, and to give to the wicked a foretaste of hell."[15]

After painting the background — the cloudy sky — Solomon focuses on the house itself. Although some details might be open to more than one interpretation, it's clear that the house represents the old person's body.

"The keepers [or guards] of the house" represent the arms and hands. In youth they are quick and strong in protecting the body. In old age they "tremble" with weakness. "The strong men" are the legs with the strongest muscles in the body. Here, too, youthful strength gives way to old age and the legs begin to "stoop."

"The grinders" in the house are the women who grind flour and prepare the food. In the body the grinders are the teeth. They stop doing their work "because they are few." Next Solomon mentions the eyes, "those looking through the windows." Again, the application is obvious. Eyesight weakens with age.

"The doors to the street" represent the ears. When they are "closed," they cut off common sounds from the outside. One of those sounds would be the grinding of grain. In spite of the loss of hearing, Solomon says old people "rise up at the sound of birds." But it's not because they hear the birds. Rather, it's because they simply can't sleep. Even though the elderly might wake up with the early birds, they can't appreciate it. For the songs of the birds are too faint.

All these debilities lead to a fear of going out. "Men are afraid of heights," afraid of falling, fearful of tripping over unseen obstacles. And there is also the fear "of dangers in the street." Lacking the strength for self-defense, many elderly people do not like to venture out into the city streets.

Following his description of the house, the Teacher now paints a blossoming almond tree into his picture of old age.

The blossoms of this tree are pink, but turn white when they are ready to fall. White hair is another sign that the end is near. Accompanying this sign of old age is the elderly's stiff, unsteady walk, represented by a grasshopper dragging himself along.

"And desire no longer is stirred." This phrase literally says, "The caperberry fails." Solomon could be referring to this food as a fruit for stimulating sexual desire, or as a spice for stimulating the desire to eat. Whatever this berry was used for, it no longer works on the old person. It fails to arouse desire. We might add other desires which fail with advancing age: the urge to learn, the many desires of the will and emotions. All desires, including even the will to live, cease.

Then the end comes. Man leaves his time-worn house of flesh and bones and moves on to his "eternal home." Perhaps the Apostle Paul had Ecclesiastes in mind when he wrote so beautifully about leaving behind our "earthly tent" and moving on to our permanent "eternal house in heaven" (2 Corinthians 5:1-10).

Meanwhile back in the village life goes on. "Mourners go about the streets." There is bitterness in this remark. Even while a person is departing this life, the professional mourners come around and dicker for the job of mourning. Jeremiah mentions this practice, "Call for the wailing women to come; send now the most skillful of them" (Jeremiah 9:17). Jesus encountered "flute players" and "people crying and wailing loudly" in the house of the girl he raised back to life (Matthew 9:23; Mark 5:38). No doubt these were the kind of paid mourners Solomon speaks of. The people of the Middle East are openly emotional and give vent to their grief through loud wailing as they walk through the streets. In ancient times hired mourners helped create the desired mood. We have our own ways of expressing grief, including the use of hired professionals to help with the funeral.

>⁶Remember him — before the silver cord is severed,
> or the golden bowl is broken;
>before the pitcher is shattered at the spring,
> or the wheel broken at the well,
>⁷and the dust returns to the ground it came from,
> and the spirit returns to God who gave it.
>⁸"Meaningless! Meaningless!" says the Teacher.
> "Everything is meaningless!"

With various figures of speech the Teacher pictures death: the cutting of a silver cord, the breaking of a golden bowl, the shattering of a clay pitcher, the breaking of a wheel. The first two images, of silver and gold, depict life's *preciousness*. Some have seen in the silver cord a reference to the spinal cord. But it's unlikely that Solomon is making any sort of anatomical statement. Rather, he is describing life as a golden lamp-bowl hanging by a silver cord. When the cord is cut, the bowl crashes to the floor and breaks.

With the pictures of the broken pitcher and wheel, the Teacher represents death as the end of life's *usefulness*. The ancients used clay pitchers to carry water from the spring or well. The wheel also served in this process. A rope running over a wheel would make it easier to draw water. The constant wearing upon the wheel would finally bring about its collapse. Shattered bits of clay and wornout wheels — more sad images of death.

With death comes a return to dust. When Solomon speaks of our bodies as dust, he recalls God's words to Adam:

> By the sweat of your brow
>   you will eat your food
> until you return to the ground,
>   since from it you were taken;
> for dust you are
>   and to dust you will return. (Genesis 3:19)

"And the spirit returns to God who gave it." This clear statement sharply contradicts those commentators who claim that Old Testament believers had no concept of life after death. Solomon has previously spoken of the judgment to come (3:17). Now in his discussion of life's end, he again asserts that each of us must someday face his Maker. God created us, giving each of us a body and soul (spirit). When your spirit returns to God, what kind of account will you give? What have you done with the life he's given you? What can you plead but the blood and merits of your Savior?

At the end of the world the body will be resurrected and rejoined to the spirit. Solomon does not speak of this. The Prophet Daniel more than alluded to it. "Multitudes who sleep in the dust of the earth will awake; some to everlasting life, others to shame and everlasting contempt" (Daniel 12:2). In general the Old Testament does not present the resurrection in the fullness in which we know it from the New Testament. Commentator H. C. Leupold has properly noted that this does not mean the Old Testament is flawed or in error:

> When we say that the doctrine of the hereafter was not revealed in all its fullness in the Old Testament we do not imply that there was any defect or error in the statement of it, or that the Old Testament statement of it was so rudimentary as to give rise to all manner of misconceptions. The same truths that the New Testament presents are offered by the Old. But the Old does not know all details of these truths as yet.[16]

Having discussed the end of life, the Teacher reiterates his theme for life under the sun: "Meaningless! Meaningless! . . . " Without God life is an empty shell. Without him there is no hope for a happy hereafter.

Life on earth is short and fleeting. Let us look beyond. Eternity stretches before us.

CONCLUSION
ECCLESIASTES 12:9-14

The shadows are lengthening across the temple courtyard as King Solomon continues his speech. He has spoken of the emptiness of life under the sun and of the fullness of life under God. In beautiful picture language he has described man's brief life on earth, before he "goes to his eternal home."

Now we sense that the king is about to tie it all together and conclude his discourse.

The Conclusion of the Matter

⁹Not only was the Teacher wise, but also he imparted knowledge to the people. He pondered and searched out and set in order many proverbs. ¹⁰The Teacher searched to find just the right words, and what he wrote was upright and true.

¹¹The words of the wise are like goads, their collected sayings like firmly embedded nails — given by one Shepherd. ¹²Be warned, my son, of anything in addition to them.

Of making many books there is no end, and much study wearies the body.

Because the Teacher here refers to himself with the third person "he" rather than using the first person "I," many commentators think that Solomon did not write the concluding verses of Ecclesiastes. But this would not be the first time Solomon has spoken this way. He used the third person in the beginning of the book (1:2) and in the middle (7:27). It's not surprising, then, that he should speak from this view-

"Not only was the Teacher wise, but also he imparted knowledge to the people."

126

point in his conclusion. The book of Nehemiah is another book in which the author speaks of himself in both ways (Nehemiah 1:1; 8:10). Christ often fluctuated between calling himself "the Son of Man" and "I," on occasion within the same sentence! (Mark 14:62)

Here Solomon says it is one thing to be wise, and another to share that wisdom with people. The Teacher shared his great wisdom. 1 Kings 4:32 informs us that Solomon "spoke three thousand proverbs." God saw to it that several hundred of them have come down through the ages in the books of Proverbs and Ecclesiastes.

Is Solomon bragging when he refers to his own wisdom? No. Throughout Ecclesiastes he has shown that everything depends upon God. When he refers to his wisdom here, he does so to make another point. Solomon wants us to be aware that his words should not be taken lightly. Far from bragging, Solomon is about to recall that his wisdom came from God himself. In Numbers 12:3 Moses spoke of himself as "a very humble man, more humble than anyone else on the face of the earth." There, too, he spoke in such a manner in order to make a point — namely, that God had chosen this lowly man to be the spokesman for the Almighty. God uses all sorts of people to be instruments of his power and wisdom. The glory belongs to the Lord and not to the human instrument.

However we might picture Solomon composing the book of Ecclesiastes, we can be sure that he was being guided by the Holy Ghost and therefore carefully chose "just the right words." The Teacher asserts that his writing (whether penned by his own hand or taken by dictation) was "upright and true." This applies to the very Word of God. His Word is truth.

The words we have received from Solomon are more than mere human opinions. They are inspired by the Lord. Solomon likens them to "goads" and "embedded nails." Goads were sharp sticks for driving oxen or used by shepherds to prod their sheep forward. Like goads, the inspired Scriptures drive people to action. God's Word pricks our conscience, pierces us to the heart, drives us to repentance and directs us to faith. While goads depict action, embedded nails symbolize stability. They hold things together and strengthen them. God's Word holds our lives together; it is our strength and stability. Indeed, it is the only solid foundation in this world of instability and change.

The words of the wise have such qualities because they are "given by one Shepherd." The Shepherd here can refer only to the Lord. Throughout the Bible God is called the Shepherd. Already in Genesis 48:15 Jacob spoke of "the God who has been my Shepherd." And Jesus the Son of God calls himself "the good shepherd" who "lays down his life for the sheep" (John 10:11). In some of the Scripture's most memorable words, Solomon's father David wrote, "The Lord is my shepherd" (Psalm 23:1).

Through the words of the Bible this Shepherd leads his people. The "wise men" of whom Solomon speaks are no other than those Peter wrote about: " . . . men spoke from God as they were carried along by the Holy Spirit" (1 Peter 1:21). These are the men to whom God gave the thoughts and words which have become the Bible. Their words are true and without error. They are from the one Shepherd.

The words from the Shepherd are to be trusted above all else. King Solomon warns against "anything in addition to them." He addresses this warning to "my son." This ancient term of endearment was commonly used by teachers for their disciples. For example, in Proverbs 3:1 Solomon says, "My son, do not forget my teaching."

Solomon's warning against adding to God's Word goes hand in hand with the Bible's caution against "false prophets" (Matthew 7:15) and against distorting the Scriptures to one's "own destruction" (2 Peter 3:16).

One need for these warnings arises from the profusion of misleading literature. Through the centuries it has remained true that "of making many books there is no end." And of the many books, most are not worth reading. This was true in Martin Luther's day five centuries ago. "For it happens that when one good book is published," remarked Luther, "ten bad ones are also published." It seems the ratio is much higher in our day.

We live in an age of tremendous advances in communication. Radio, movies, television, telephone, video, tape recorders and other products of modern technology have combined to make communication faster and easier than our ancestors ever dreamed possible. Along with this the book industry flourishes as never before. In the United States about 50,000 new books are published each year. As many as a third of them are religious publications.

We are flooded with communication of all sorts. Some of it is obvious trash. Much of it is misleading. With all kinds of messages bombarding us and with so much to read, it is especially important that we don't neglect the one thing needful, the Word of God. The Christian will try to devote time to reading the Bible and good books which aid the study of God's Word. Luther offered some good advice as to how we might go about our reading:

> A student who does not want his labor wasted must so read and reread some good writer that the author is changed, as it were, into his flesh and blood. For a great variety of reading confuses and does not teach. It makes the student like a man who dwells everywhere and, therefore, nowhere in particular. Just as we do not daily enjoy the society of every one of our friends but only that of a chosen few, so it should also be in our studying.[17]

129

"Much study wearies the body," adds Solomon. Here Solomon is not speaking of the study of Scripture. This is clear from his placement of the remark at the end of this section, immediately after his warning against making additions to God's Word. It is also clear from other parts of Scripture. While the philosophies and entertainments of the world become wearisome, God's Word does not. The righteous man "meditates day and night" on God's Word (Psalm 1:2). It renews him, strengthens him, and sets his heart free (Psalm 119:25-32).

> ¹³**Now all has been heard;**
> **here is the conclusion of the matter:**
> **Fear God and keep his commandments,**
> **for this is the whole duty of man.**
> ¹⁴**For God will bring every deed into judgment,**
> **including every hidden thing,**
> **whether it is good or evil.**

Through all of Ecclesiastes Solomon has been building toward his conclusion. Now he presents it. This is how to live amid the vanity of the world. This is how to overcome a meaningless existence. "Fear God."

The Hebrew word translated "fear" denotes much more than terror. It carries the ideas of respect, awe and reverence. As a matter of fact, those who fear God are delivered from all terror! David declared,

> I sought the Lord, and he answered me;
> he delivered me from all my fears. . . .
> The angel of the Lord encamps
> around those who fear him,
> and he delivers them. . . .
> Fear the Lord, you his saints,
> for those who fear him lack nothing.
> (Psalm 34:4,7,9)

At times, "fear" is closely associated with "trust," as when David wrote in another Psalm: "Many will see and fear and put their trust in the Lord" (Psalm 40:30). All of these concepts are present in Solomon's words, "Fear God!" Trust in God. Everything is in his hands. In his love he will care for you.

Where there is fear of God, there is also a desire to keep his commandments. "To fear the Lord is to hate evil" (Proverbs 8:13). Out of respect for God, believers want to do only what pleases him.

This, says Solomon, is what life is all about. It is our "whole duty" during life. Life has no other purpose than to seek God's glory.

Perhaps to some the Teacher's conclusion appears to be simplistic. It sounds like something a five-year-old might repeat to his Sunday school teacher. Yet the wisest man in the world deems it the highest course of wisdom. "Fear God."

Such is the nature of the Christian faith. It may be child-like and simple. Nevertheless, it is the way of salvation.

In Ecclesiastes Solomon has said much about God's goodness and his gifts to men. Several times he has also mentioned the reality of the judgment to come. In an abrupt way he now ends the book on the same note of judgment. St. Paul twice referred to the closing verse of Ecclesiastes in his letters to the Corinthians. "He [the Lord] will bring to light what is hidden in darkness and will expose the motives of men's hearts. At that time each will receive his praise from God" (1 Corinthians 4:5). "For we must all appear before the judgment seat of Christ, that each one may receive what is due him for the things done while in the body, whether good or bad" (2 Corinthians 5:10).

That Solomon should end his book with a word of judgment has disturbed some scholars. As they made copies of Ecclesiastes, Jewish scribes often would repeat the second last verse at the end to create a happier ending. (They did the same thing with Isaiah, Lamentations and Malachi.) But that was unnecessary. The God-fearing child of God does not need to fear the judgment. He knows that in his Savior he will find forgiveness, even for his "hidden faults" (Psalm 19:12).

So there is nothing more to life — and nothing less! —than this: Fear God! Follow him and his Word. He will lead you through this world. He will lead you through the judgment. He will lead you beyond the sun and into eternal glory.

These closing verses of Ecclesiastes are the words of a repentant man. Quite possibly they are Solomon's last recorded words. The final historical description of Solomon in the book of Kings does not mention his tragic lapse into sin. Instead, it commends "the wisdom he displayed" (1 Kings 11:41).

Then it goes on to say that "he rested with his fathers and was buried in the city of David his father" (1 Kings 11:43).

We can thank God that before going to his rest King Solomon left us with the book of Ecclesiastes. In this marvelous portion of Scripture he has demonstrated that life can be lived in only two ways — without God or with God. We don't have to look far to see the futility of the former. By God's grace we have come to know him as our Savior. Whenever possible, let us share our life under God with others. Our gift can become theirs. The time we have in this life is short. Soon the silver cord will be severed. Soon the spirit will return to God who gave it. And soon we, too, shall rest with our fathers.

The years rush by quickly. Many generations have lived and died in the twenty-nine centuries since Solomon's time. But the sun still rises and sets over Jerusalem. The wind still swirls across the ancient hills around that timeless city. The streams continue to flow into the sea. Man still toils under the burning sun.

Meanwhile, the words of the Teacher, son of David, king
in Jerusalem, live on.

    "Meaningless! Meaningless!
     says the Teacher.
    "Utterly meaningless!
     Everything is meaningless."
    . . . .
    Now all has been heard;
     here is the conclusion of the matter:
    Fear God and keep his commandments,
     for this is the whole duty of man.

Jewish Bride

SONG OF SONGS
INTRODUCTION

Name and Author

The book's name is taken from the opening verse, "Solomon's Song of Songs." Besides the title *Song of Songs*, the book is also known as the *Song of Solomon* or *Canticle*, a Latin word meaning song.

The term "Song of Songs" is a Hebrew superlative. It means "the best of songs" or, as one translation puts it, "the most beautiful of songs." This type of expression is common in the Hebrew of the Old Testament. We think, for example, of expressions like "Lord of lords" (that is, the greatest Lord), "holy of holies" (the most holy place in the tabernacle and temple), "vanities of vanities" (the greatest vanity; translated in the NIV as "Meaningless! Meaningless!"). The Song of Songs is a special book.

The opening verse attributes the song to Solomon. Either he personally wrote it or it belonged to him and was a part of his royal collection of literature. Much of modern scholarship denies the Solomonic authorship of this book, just as it does for Ecclesiastes. The main argument is that the poem contains a number of Aramaic words, which supposedly would date the book several centuries after Solomon's time. As has already been noted in the Introduction to Ecclesiastes, this is not a very convincing argument. It is part of a general trend to assign many of the books of Scripture later dates than the Bible itself would allow.

This writer accepts the traditional authorship — that of Solomon. The first verse strongly suggests this. And the contents speak of Solomon. Moreover, the Bible says that Solomon wrote many songs. "He spoke three thousand proverbs and his songs numbered a thousand and five" (1 Kings 4:32).

The Song is filled with references to plant life (nineteen plants mentioned) and animals (thirteen). This coincides with Solomon's vast knowledge of flora and fauna. 1 Kings 4:33 relates how King Solomon "described plant life, from the cedar of Lebanon to the hyssop that grows out of walls. He also taught about animals and birds, reptiles and fish." The writer's obvious familiarity with many expensive materials such as ivory and precious stones also points to the wealthy monarch as the author.

A number of Solomon's writings are a part of God's inspired Word: Song of Songs, Proverbs, Ecclesiastes and Psalms 72 and 127. According to ancient tradition, the Song of Songs is a product of Solomon's youth, Proverbs of his middle age and Ecclesiastes of his old age. The content of these books seems to bear this out.

Place in the Bible

The Song of Songs was one of the Megilloth, the five books read each year during the Jewish festivals. The Song of Songs was used for the Passover. This festival commemorated the Israelite's deliverance from bondage in Egypt. Although the book describes the love between a man and woman, it is also picturing the love between God and his people. Such a theme would certainly be appropriate for the Passover.

Interestingly, it was during the time of the Passover that Jesus often alluded to the bride and bridegroom theme: the parables of the marriage feast (Matthew 22:1-14) and of the ten virgins (Matthew 25:1-13); his discussion concerning marriage and the resurrection (Matthew 22:23-33); and his words of farewell to his disciples, "I am going to prepare a place for you" (John 14:1-4). This last reference is an allusion to the custom of the bridegroom preparing a place for his bride and then coming back to take her. Whether all these references spring directly from the Song of Songs, which was read at that time of year, we cannot be certain.

The entire Song is poetry and perhaps was originally set to music. In our English Bibles it is one of the five poetical books. Our Introduction to Ecclesiastes includes a discussion of biblical poetry. The poetical books are at times also classified as wisdom literature.

Interpretation

The Song is a short book. It can be read aloud in less than twenty minutes. Despite its brevity the book has proved the source of endless discussion.

That may sound surprising. In our day the Song of Songs is probably one of the least preached about and least read books in the entire Bible. How many sermons have you heard from this book, or how many of its passages have you memorized? While Solomon's Song may be neglected on some levels, it continues to be perhaps the most written-about book in the Old Testament. And if we were to put together all the literature of previous centuries — as one commentator observed, "A thorough study of the history of the interpretation of the Canticles would require the lifelong labor of teams of scholars."[1]

A prime reason for the vast amount of material on the Song (and for the lack of its popular usage) is the difficulty of the book's interpretation. To quote from another scholar, the Song of Solomon is the "most obscure book in the Old Testament."[2]

There are three basic interpretations of the Song, with many variations on these three.

The first is the *literal* (sometimes called the secular) interpretation. According to this view, Solomon's Song simply describes the love between a man and a woman. Although this view was already suggested as early as A.D. 300, it has become especially popular in our age of secularism and rationalism, which exalts human thoughts and sentiments.

Under the canopy of this secular interpretation there are many variations. Some see in the poem more than just the love between Solomon and the Shulammite shepherdess. They find a love triangle, the chief characters being Solomon, the shepherd girl and a shepherd. Others consider the book to be a song written to commemorate the wedding of Solomon to the daughter of Pharoah (1 Kings 3:1). We shall discuss these views in our commentary on 1:7 and 1:9. Still others view the book as a collection of wedding poems. And some have claimed that the book consists of ancient Canaanite love poetry used in fertility rites.

The literal approach runs into two problems. For one thing, if the Song is merely secular, what is it doing in the Bible? Although its presence in Scripture has been questioned on occasion, the Song's acceptance goes back to ancient times. Jewish rabbis as well as the early Christians recognized the book as part of God's Word. Because it is part of the inspired Scriptures, the book should in some way point to Christ. Our Savior asserts that all the Scriptures "testify" of him (John 5:39). A book which does not rise above the theme of human love may be valuable, but has little part in the Bible, which is "able to make you wise for salvation through faith in Christ Jesus" (2 Timothy 3:15). A high view of Scripture rules out the notion that the Song is merely love poetry, especially poetry used in Canaanite fertility rites!

The other problem with the literal or secular interpretation is that it does not fit all the details of the book. While at first glance the Canticle might strike one as nothing more than a love poem, closer examination reveals details which hint at meanings beyond a literal explanation. For example, at times the "daughters of Jerusalem" (2:7) are addressed in the masculine gender; this is an indication that the Song is here referring to people in general and not just to the women.

A second main approach to the book is the *typical* interpretation. What this means in biblical interpretation is that there is a real person, event, office or institution from the Old Testament which foreshadows, or is a type of, a person, event, office or institution in the New Testament, which is its antitype (the thing itself). For instance, the serpent of bronze (Numbers 21:4-9) was a type of Christ (John 3:14-16); Christ is the antitype. Just as the serpent was lifted up on a pole, so Jesus was raised up on a cross. And just as those who looked at the bronze snake were spared from death, so all who look to Christ in faith are spared from eternal death in hell.

If we interpret the Song of Songs in this manner, Solomon becomes a type of Christ. Similar to the literal approach, this interpretation sees the book as a love story. According to the typical interpretation, the Song relates the love between Solomon and the maiden. But the typical intrepretation takes it a step farther: just as Solomon loved the poor country girl, so Christ loves his church. The poem, then, has two meanings, the literal and the typical. While this approach explains the book's presence in Scripture, it runs into the problem of not conforming to actual history. As we shall see, Solomon does not fit the poem's description of him as a shepherd.

The third main class of interpretation is the *allegorical*, or spiritual. An allegory is a story in which the people and events, which may or may not be real, have hidden or symbolic meanings. With this approach the literal understanding recedes into the background and sometimes is completely dropped. There is little or no attempt to relate the Canticle to history, to Solomon or to any particular human relationship. Instead, a spiritual meaning is read into the Song from beginning to end. Over the years this has been the most popular method of interpreting the book. Ancient Jewish rabbis saw the Canticle as the story of God's love for his chosen people Israel. Many Christians see in it the love between Christ and his church. Luther treated the Song as a picture of the relation between God's appointed rulers (Solomon) and the people (the maiden). Others have seen the book as representing wisdom and those who seek wisdom.

The allegorical interpretation has much to commend it. For one thing, it doesn't stumble over any difficulties with the literal meanings of words and passages. Nor is there a need for the poem to conform to real history. Furthermore, if used to point to God and Christ, the Song does indeed fit into the flow of Scripture as it reveals God's love.

Nor is this approach to the Song alien to the rest of Scripture. When Moses wrote the first books of the Bible, he used the husband-wife relationship to represent God and his people. Moses frequently compared unfaithfulness to God with marital unfaithfulness (see Exodus 34:14-16; Leviticus 20:5,6; Deuteronomy 31:16). The prophets who lived after Solomon closely tied God's relation with Israel to the relation between husband and wife. Isaiah, for example wrote, "As a bridegroom rejoices over his bride, so will your God rejoice over you" (Isaiah 62:5). As we go through the Song we'll look at other such passages from the prophets. Psalm 45, "A Song of Love," parallels the Song of Songs in many ways. It describes the wedding of a king, who is referred to as a man and as God himself (verses 6,7). Hebrews 1:8,9 quotes these verses and applies them to Jesus Christ. Other New Testament passages take up this theme and refer to Christ as the bridegroom (Matthew 9:16) and the church as his bride (Revelation 21:2).

In spite of all this the allegorical interpretation of the Canticle has one major drawback. Interpreters who follow this approach have tended to ignore the actual text and to read almost anything into it. Yet the fact remains that the Song does describe the love between a man and a woman. The fact also remains that at times the poem speaks of Solomon in very concrete terms. It's difficult to ignore the impression that at least parts of the Song are drawn from real events in the life of Solomon.

Perhaps at this point a brief review will help clarify the three main interpretations of the Song of Songs:

Literal: a poem about human love.

Typical: a poem recounting an historical human love story which is a type of the love between God and his people.

Allegorical: a poem using human love to symbolize the love between God and his people.

We've seen that each of these approaches reflects some truth. Each also has its drawbacks. Obviously Solomon's Song does not fit neatly into any single classification. Throughout the centuries the Song has risen above commentators' attempts to squeeze it into this or that literary genre.

Rather than trying to categorize it, it seems best to let the book speak for itself in the light of the rest of Scripture. The book speaks of love and marriage. At the same time it is impossible to speak of these subjects without reference to Christ, the heavenly bridegroom, and his love for us. For Christians these are not unrelated subjects. In the beginning God himself instituted marriage (Genesis 2:18-25). He designed this institution with himself at the center. Only where God and his forgiving love are present can marriage come close to what he intends it to be.

The poem, then, has a double meaning "built in." It speaks of human love, often drawing from Solomon's personal experience. But it also points to another love, that between Christ and his people.

Whether married or not, we will appreciate the beauty of Solomon's most excellent Song. And whether married or not, we can enjoy the love of the heavenly bridegroom Jesus Christ.

Outline

The Song has been outlined in many ways. Almost every commentator has his own idea as to where and how to divide the poem. As was the case with Ecclesiastes, there are two main schools of thought in regard to the book's structure. Some believe that the Song is not really one poem, but a collection of many. One commentator divides the Song into twenty-nine short love poems! Others, including this writer, are convinced the entire Song is a unit.

While it is not always easy to follow the book's transitions from one part to another, there are excellent reasons for taking it as a single poem. The title calls it the Song, not songs. Common phrases appear throughout the book. For example, the expression, "Do not arouse or awaken love until it so desires" occurs several times (2:7; 3:5; 8:4). The same chief characters — Solomon, the shepherdess, the friends — appear in the entire poem. We can also trace a progression of thought from beginning to end. The Song starts with courtship, moves on to the wedding ceremony, then shows the couple struggling through a brief time of separation, and finally ends with them happily reminiscing.

Following this progression and taking the book as a single poem, we can divide the Song into these four sections:

> The Springtime of Love (1:1—3:5)
> The Wedding (3:6—5:1)

Separation and Reunion (5:2-8:4)
Reminiscences (8:5-14)

With this background information, we will proceed to the Song itself. Drink in the magnificent poetry and take to heart the message of this, the most beautiful of songs.

Gazelles in the Hill Country of Israel

THE SPRINGTIME OF LOVE
SONG OF SONGS 1:1—3:5

The winter rains have ended. Blossoms cover the trees and hillsides. Spring has come. It is a time for love.

1 Solomon's Song of Songs.

Beloved

²Let him kiss me with the kisses of his mouth —
for your love is more delightful than wine.
³Pleasing is the fragrance of your perfumes;
your name is like perfume poured out.
No wonder the maidens love you!
⁴Take me away with you — let us hurry!
The king has brought me into his chambers.

The book's opening verse is really its title. This was discussed in the Introduction.

Following the title we hear the voice of the first speaker, the "Beloved." The designations of speakers are not in the original text, but have been added by the translators. The NIV translators supply this note to explain how they determined who the speakers are: "Primarily on the basis of the gender of the Hebrew pronouns used, male and female speakers are indicated in the margins by the captions *Lover* and *Beloved* respectively. The words of others are marked *Friends*. In some instances the divisions and their captions are debatable."

It's obvious from her opening words that the beloved is in love with her lover. Whether or not he is present with her at the

145

moment is unclear. She refers to him indirectly, "Let him kiss me. . . . " Yet she also speaks as if he were with her, " . . . your love. . . . " When people love each other they are always with each other, even when they are apart. He is always on her mind and in her heart. And she is intoxicated with his love, which "is more delightful than wine."

His "perfumes" or oils — we might call them colognes — are fragrant. "Your name (*shem*) is like perfume (*shemen*)!" she exclaims. Even to hear his name is thrilling. Everything about him delights her!

Nor is she the only one who is overcome at the thought of this man. "The maidens" also love him. The word translated "maidens" is the same word Isaiah used to describe the mother of the Savior, "The *virgin* will be with child . . . " (Isaiah 7:14).

The King James Version translates the opening line of verse 4, "Draw me, we will run after thee." This translation is more in keeping with the ancient reading of this verse. And it is the first of a number of passages which in various ways hint at something beyond a literal love story taking place in the Song of Songs. It would hardly be natural for a girl to want to run off with her beloved *and* a crowd of others. Wouldn't she want to be alone with the king? But if the King represents Christ, then it makes sense. Believers want others to join them in following Jesus.

Understood in this way, the line is the theme for a beautiful old Ascension hymn, depicting the believers' love for their Savior:

> Draw us to thee,
> For then shall we
>   Walk in thy steps forever
> And hasten on
> Where thou art gone
>   To be with thee dear Savior.

Jesus himself spoke in a similar fashion when he said, "I . . . will draw all men to myself" (John 12:32).

Suddenly the beloved declares, "Let the king bring me into his chambers." She longs to be in the home of the one she loves, just as we long to be with Christ.

Friends
> We rejoice and delight in you;
> we will praise your love more than wine.

Beloved
> How right they are to adore you!
> 5Dark am I, yet lovely,
> O daughters of Jerusalem,
> dark like the tents of Kedar,
> like the tent curtains of Solomon.
> 6Do not stare at me because I am dark,
> because I am darkened by the sun.
> My mother's sons were angry with me
> and made me take care of the vineyards;
> my own vineyard I have neglected.

The friends, also referred to in the Song as the "daughters of Jerusalem" (1:5), now chime in. They echo the beloved's admiration for her lover: "We rejoice and delight in you." The Hebrew for "you" is masculine singular, referring to the lover. They also compare his love to wine.

The beloved commends her friends' good taste: "How right they are to adore you!" One commentator observes that this is what every young woman should be able to say about the man she intends to marry:

> A girl today should be able to say the same things about the boy she may someday marry. Generally speaking, she should not be the only person in the world who sees what a good person her potential mate is. She should not be so infatu-

ated that she imagines a scoundrel or knave to be her knight in shining armor. She should be able to say, "rightly do I love you." He should be the kind of person one ought to respect. For if he is not, she may find it much more difficult to respond to his leadership.[3]

As special and worthy of admiration as her lover is, the beloved can only wonder, "What does he see in me?" This is a natural feeling for people in love. They are painfully aware of their own imperfections and find it hard to imagine how the object of their affection could care for them.

The young lady proceeds to enumerate her shortcomings to her friends. She is "dark like the tents of Kedar." Her dark, swarthy complexion stands in sharp contrast to the fair-skinned girls of the palace. Today a dark tan is often a sign of wealth, leisure and beauty. For the ancients it was just the opposite. The wealthy and the nobility stayed out of the sun, while the lower class people were forced to work out in the open. To be darkened by the sun symbolized work and frequently poverty for the ancients. The Bible pictures heaven itself as an escape from toil under the sun — "The sun will not beat upon them, nor any scorching heat" (Revelation 7:16).

The term "Kedar" refers to the nomads or Bedouin tribes, in particular those who lived in the area south-east of Damascus. They were descendants of Kedar, a son of Abraham's son Ishmael (Genesis 25:13). The girl likens her complexion to the nomad tents which were (and still are) covered with dark goats' hair. She was familiar with Kedar and the nomads of that region, because, as the poem will indicate, she was from the area nearby.

Her comparison to "the tent curtains of Solomon," which must also have been dark, is a second reference to her darkness. Then she expresses her desire that others not stare at her "because I am dark." Obviously her darkness bothered her quite a bit.

And yet she calls herself "lovely"! How can this be? She knows that in her lover's sight she is lovely. He sees in her nothing but beauty and grace. Throughout the poem he describes her with terms such as, "most beautiful of women" (1:8), "a lily among thorns" (2:2), "my dove" (2:14), "my darling" (4:1), "lovely" (6:4). They say that love is blind. In this case, however, it is not a matter of blindness but of his overlooking her shortcomings.

This is a wonderful example for people contemplating marriage today — an openness about their own shortcomings and a willingness to overlook those in their future mate. Such attitudes remind us of the fruits which the gospel produces in Christians. Though we are scorched and scarred by sin, in Christ's eyes we are beautiful. "Though your sins are like scarlet, they shall be as white as snow," declares the Lord, "though they are red as crimson, they shall be like wool" (Isaiah 1:18). Confident of Christ's love and forgiveness, we can love and forgive one another.

From her appearance the beloved turns to her other problems. "My mother's sons were angry with me." Because she does not directly call them her brothers, they may have been her stepbrothers. In their anger they made her tend their vineyards. We are not told why they were angry. We are told that as she worked in their vineyards she neglected her own.

The Bible makes frequent reference to the vineyard, often comparing it to things spiritual. We shall look into this more in the last chapter where the vineyard theme comes up again (8:11,12). Many allegorical commentators relate the vineyard here to the church. Tending the vineyard means continuing faithful in God's Word. The girl's remark about neglecting her vineyard then becomes a confession of sin. It's not hard to apply this is to our Christian life. We must confess that all too often we have failed to do what we should have done.

Scorched by the sun, mistreated by her brothers, unable to keep up with her work, this humble farm girl longs for comfort and support from the man she loves, the king himself. But she does not address him as a king. Instead she speaks of him as a shepherd:

> ⁷Tell me, you whom I love, where you graze your flock
> and where you rest your sheep at midday.
> Why should I be like a veiled woman
> beside the flocks of your friends?

As with many other passages in the Song, people have seen a great variety of meanings in this reference to the shepherd-lover. It might be worthwhile to pause for a moment and look at some of the interpretations of this verse. They help crystallize some of the basic approaches to the Song of Songs.

Some see in the poem a love triangle: the simple country girl in love with a shepherd, King Solomon in love with the girl and trying unsuccessfully to win her affection, and the shepherd who also loves the girl. This approach does away with the need to explain why Solomon is called a shepherd. But is also necessitates reading a great deal between the lines. For example, later in chapter 1 there is an exchange between the king and the maiden. He says, "We will make you earrings of gold . . . " (1:11, obviously these are not the words of a poor shepherd). She replies, "My lover is to me a sachet of myrrh" (1:13). Although she is addressing the king, we would have to surmise that she is using a sort of double-talk and *really* talking about her real lover, the shepherd. Sound complicated? It is. The so-called "shepherd hypothesis" adds so many complications to the Song that it cannot stand up.

150

This verse also presents problems for a strictly historical understanding of the Song. The fact is Solomon was not a shepherd. His father David had been a shepherd in his youth, but not Solomon. Yet throughout the Song, Solomon is not just compared to a shepherd but actually called a shepherd.

If we apply this verse to God, it fits very well. He is both King and Shepherd. Centuries before Solomon's time, Jacob had spoken of God as "the Shepherd" (Genesis 49:24). Solomon's father had declared, "The Lord is my shepherd" (Psalm 23:1). And centuries after Solomon, the Son of God would say, "I am the good shepherd" (John 10:11).

The beloved wants to be with her lover, even when he is out with the sheep. So she asks where she might find him grazing his flock and resting it at midday. With this request she displays her modesty, as she adds, "Why should I be like a veiled woman . . . ?" A veiled woman was a prostitute or at the very least an improperly aggressive woman. With her face behind a veil she would solicit men or roam about without a proper escort. It was with a veil that Tamar disguised herself as a prostitute and seduced her father-in-law Judah (Genesis 38). In many parts of the Middle East women still wear veils, not as a cover for immorality but as a sign of modesty. For a Middle Eastern woman to go out alone, veiled or not, is considered immodest, except in the larger, westernized cities.

The beloved does not want to wander around and have to ask her lover's friends where she might find him. What would they think of her? What would they think of him for causing his beloved to rove through the hills in search of him? Even in our modern, liberal society, modesty is still appropriate for Christian young people. The Apostle Paul's words apply to Christians of all ages, "Among you there must not be even a hint of sexual immorality, or of any kind of impurity . . . because these are improper for God's holy people" (Ephesians 5:3). St. Peter speaks to Christian women in particular when he says, "Your beauty should not come from outward adornment. . . . Instead, it should be that of your inner self, the unfading beauty of a gentle and quiet spirit, which is of great worth in God's sight" (1 Peter 3:3,4).

This is not to say that Christian women cover their faces or never go out alone. But regardless of where they live or what they do, God asks both Christian men and women to conduct themselves in a chaste and proper manner. This spirit of modesty and purity pervades the Song of Songs.

Friends
> ⁸If you do not know, most beautiful of women,
>   follow the tracks of the sheep
> and graze your young goats
>   by the tents of the shepherds.

Lover
> ⁹I liken you, my darling, to a mare
>   harnessed to one of the chariots of Pharaoh.
> ¹⁰Your cheeks are beautiful with earrings,
>   your neck with strings of jewels.
> ¹¹We will make you earrings of gold,
>   studded with silver.⁴

Here the friends address the lovely country maiden — "most beautiful of women." They tell her that she can find her lover among the shepherds.

Then for the first time the lover speaks. He gives no clue as to how or where he met the country girl. None of that seems to matter. What is important is the love they share. The maiden's concerns about her appearance, her problems and her finding him — all melt away as he speaks. She knows he cares about her, finds her beautiful and will be there when she needs him.

The king begins by paying her a very unusual compliment: "I liken you . . . to a mare." No girl today would be swept off her feet by such a line! Yet a compliment it was. Several pairs of horses pulled the chariots, but the prize mare was out in front. More graceful, beautiful and noble then all the others, she stood out from the crowd.

Some see in this reference to "the chariots of Pharaoh" a clue to the poem's background. Early in his reign Solomon confirmed an alliance with the Egyptian Pharaoh by marrying his daughter (1 Kings 3:1). Apparently Solomon was very fond of this wife, for he built a special palace for her (1 Kings 7:8). Nevertheless, the girl in the Song of Songs hardly fits the description of a Pharaoh's daughter. So Solomon's reference to the Egyptian chariots must be just that, a passing reference for the sake of comparison. King Solomon himself was well supplied with "fourteen hundred chariots and twelve thousand horses" (1 King 10:26). These horses were "imported from Egypt and from all other countries" (2 Chronicles 9:28). The fact that Egypt is singled out and that Solomon uses it in his comparison indicates that Egyptian horses must have been considered the cream of the crop.

The beloved is a shepherdess and vineyard worker, but she is bedecked with earrings and jewels from the king. He promises to continue to lavish her with gold and silver jewelry. Solomon could well afford this because of his fabulous wealth. Although plural, the expression "We will make . . . " can refer to the king. He is speaking for himself and his artisans who will do the actual work.

Again we cannot but notice a spiritual parallel. We are poor and spiritually bankrupt. We have nothing to offer God. But in his love he furnishes us with the most priceless things to wear. In the words of Isaiah, "I delight greatly in the Lord; my soul rejoices in my God. For he has clothed me with the garments of salvation and arrayed me in a robe of righteousness" (Isaiah 61:10).

The words, "We will make," bring to mind the words of the triune God in the opening chapter of the Bible. When God created man, the Almighty said, "Let us make man in our image, in our likeness" (Genesis 1:26). There the plural allows us to overhear the inner counsels of the three persons of the Trinity — Father, Son and Holy Ghost.

Beloved

12 While the king was at his table,
    my perfume spread its fragrance,
13 My lover is to me a sachet of myrrh
    resting between my breasts.
14 My lover is to me a cluster of henna blossoms
    from the vineyards of En Gedi.

The beloved refers back to a visit she had made to the king's palace. She talks about sitting at a banquet table. But what comes to mind is not food. Rather, it is the heady fragrance of air filled with love and perfume. Earlier she had praised his perfume (1:3); now she describes her own. She mentions three different types.

The first, simply translated "perfume," is nard or spikenard. This was imported from India. Mary of Bethany anointed Jesus with a year's wages worth of this expensive ointment (Mark 14:3-9; John 12:1-8).

Next the beloved speaks of "a sachet of myrrh." A woman of means wore a little cloth bag of this costly resin. Wherever she went the fragrance went with her. In the same way her lover was in her heart wherever she went. Myrrh was one of the wise men's gifts to the Christ Child (Matthew 2:11).

Thirdly, she mentions "henna blossoms." When crushed, the leaves of this shrub produce an orange dye used as a hair coloring or on the fingernails. The small white flowers of this plant give off a sweet fragrance.

En Gedi was and remains a luxuriant oasis on the western shore of the Dead Sea. To the beloved the king is like an oasis in the desert.

Exotic fragrances, beautiful settings — these are the images of the Song of Songs.

Lover
> [15]How beautiful you are, my darling!
>   Oh, how beautiful!
>   Your eyes are doves.

Beloved
> [16]How handsome you are, my lover!
>   Oh, how charming!
>   And our bed is verdant.

Lover
> [17]The beams of our house are cedars;
>   our rafters are firs.

The exchange between lover and beloved continues with short exclamations of mutual admiration and affection.

He reassures her that he thinks she is beautiful. And then he says it once more, "Oh, how beautiful!" He is especially infatuated with her eyes. He doesn't say, "They are like doves," but, "Your eyes *are* doves." Gentle, fluttering, lively and pure. It is interesting that Job named one of his daughters Jemimah (Job 42:14), a Hebrew word for dove. Still more interesting is the fact that the Holy Spirit chose to appear as a dove at Jesus' baptism (Matthew 3:16). No doubt this says something of the nature of the Spirit, who has been called "the shy member of the Trinity." In his pure and gentle manner the Spirit works within the hearts of people, directing them not to himself but to Jesus. Christians, too, says Jesus, are to be "as innocent as doves" (Matthew 10:16).

The beloved coos to the king, "How handsome you are. . . . " In Hebrew she uses the same word he used to describe her, translated "beautiful" in the previous verse. The exchange between the two is something like this: He says, "You are comely." And she responds, "No, *you* are comely." One compliment is never quite enough for these two, and so she quickly adds, "Oh, how charming!" This is the same basic word used by Moses in Psalm 90:17 (KJV): "And let the *beauty* of the Lord our God be upon us."

The girl's love for the country shines through as she hurriedly gets in one more thought, "And our bed [or couch] is verdant." Her heart is not in cities and palaces but in the luxurious green hills of the north. There in the great outdoors she can recline with the one she loves.

The lover takes up this thought and exclaims, "The beams of our house are cedar; our rafters are firs." While she might be thinking of tree branches beneath the open sky, the king apparently has in mind his palace back in Jerusalem. With "cedar columns supporting trimmed cedar beams" (1 Kings 7:2), the structure was known as "the Palace of the Forest of Lebanon." Wood was scarce in Palestine and was imported for exclusive building projects.

Although they are not yet married, he speaks of "our" house. What is his he wants to share with her.

Beloved
2   **I am a rose of Sharon,
a lily of the valleys.**
Lover
    **²Like a lily among thorns
is my darling among the maidens.**

It seems the maiden has caught the king's allusion to his palace. She banters back that she is just a country girl. She likens herself to a wild meadow flower — a crocus, or a rose.

(It is uncertain exactly which flower is meant by the Hebrew word.) These flowers grow in the plain of Sharon along the Mediterranean coast of Israel.

As in English, the Hebrew first person does not indicate gender. The pronoun "I" could refer either to the man or woman. Some old church symbols depict Christ as the Rose of Sharon, thus making the king (representing Christ) the subjects of verse 1. It's more likely, however, that it refers to the girl, since this better catches the flow of the conversation.

In poetic parallelism to the rose of Sharon, the beloved proceeds to liken herself to a flower found in the valleys. Not to be confused with what we call the lily of the valley, the flower she alludes to was more likely a water lily. Perhaps this lily was a popular subject of the song writer. Psalm 45, a wedding song with many similarities to the Song of Solomon, has in its heading the note: "To the tune of 'Lilies.' "

The girl's shyness is evident in her choice of the rose and the lily. She likens herself to two ordinary wildflowers, often overlooked on the plain and hidden in the valleys.

Her lover teases her, "Yes, you are a lily — a lily among thorns!" In his eyes other women cannot compare to his beloved. Just as beautiful flowers spring up in the swampy plain or rough valleys, so his flower has sprung up where he would least expect to find her.

Beloved
> ³Like an apple tree among the trees of the forest
>   is my lover among the young men.
> I delight to sit in his shade,
>   and his fruit is sweet to my taste.
> ⁴He has taken me to the banquet hall,
>   and his banner over me is love.
> ⁵Strengthen me with raisins,
>   refresh me with apples,
>   for I am faint with love.

> [6]His left arm is under my head,
>   and his right arm embraces me.
> [7]Daughters of Jerusalem, I charge you
>   by the gazelles and by the does of the field:
> Do not arouse or awaken love
>   until it so desires.

After the lovers' quick give-and-take, the beloved now launches into an extensive monologue. Here we might imagine a change of scenes, since she is not speaking to him but about him.

Again she draws her comparisons from nature. He is "like an apple tree" compared with the wild trees of the forest which bear no worthwhile fruit. She continues the picture as she speaks of her delight "to sit in his shade." "Shade," or "shadow," symbolizes protection. For example, the psalmist states, "The Lord watches over you — the Lord is your shade at your right hand; the sun will not harm you by day, nor the moon by night" (Psalm 121:5,6). As God protects his people, he expects Christian men to protect and care for their women — to be their shade.

The beloved continues to draw on the apple-tree comparison and exclaims how she delights in "his fruits." Not only is he her life and protection, but also her sustinence. He provides for her needs.

It seems that her talk about the apple tree has turned her thoughts to food, as she suddenly shifts from the outdoors to the banquet hall (literally, "the house of wine"). Here again the tone is one of modesty and propriety. This banquet hall setting is quite unlike that described in an ancient Egyptian love song: "Her lover sitteth at her right hand. The feast is disordered with drunkenness."[5]

In the hall hangs the king's royal banner, just as the tribes of Israel had their unique banners (Numbers 1:52). The king's standard, or banner, was highly visible, a sign of his presence. Like a banner, the king's love for the maiden is evident to all.

Faint with love, she calls out for nourishment. Some commentators who follow the secular interpretation see here an erotic reference to ancient Canaanite fertility rites. The apples and raisins supposedly served as aphrodisiacs. The heathen often connected the eating of raisin cakes with their immoral worship (see Hosea 3:1). While there certainly is no need to see references to pagan worship here, it could well be that the beloved's mention of apples and raisins expresses something other than a call for actual food. It may very well allude to her desire for the love of the king. His love is her source of nourishment and strength.

The New American Standard Bible and some other translations render verse 6 as a wish — "Let his left hand be under my head and his right hand embrace me." But the NIV's direct statement is a more accurate translation. The lover comes to her in her weakness and embraces her. He is her strength. Similarly, St. Peter urges husbands, "Be considerate as you live with your wives, and treat them with respect as the weaker partner" (1 Peter 3:7). Without depicting one or the other as inferior or superior, the Bible regularly points to the man as the leader. We see this strong yet considerate quality in the lover in the Song of Songs.

The closing verse of this section will occur two more times in the poem (3:5; 8:4). On each occasion it marks a shift in the story line. Although every verse in the Song is rich with imagery, this verse is especially fascinating. Some contend that the lover is speaking here. Nevertheless, because the beloved speaks the verses immediately preceding and following, it's most likely that these words are also hers.

She addresses the daughters of Jerusalem, but when she uses the word "you" it is maculine! This is another hint at another level of meaning; the beloved is not just speaking to women. Back in 1:4 we noted how the maidens following the king could depict the believers in general. Here, too, we can see in the daughters of Jerusalem a reference to the church. Often Scripture speaks of God's people as Jerusalem. Hebrews 12:22,23, for instance, refers to the church in heaven as "the heavenly Jerusalem."

The daughters of Jerusalem are addressed as though being asked to take an oath. According to Deuteronomy 6:13, if people took an oath it was to be done in God's name. But here they are charged (KJV, "adjure") by "the gazelles and the does of the field." This is probably a play on words. The Hebrew words for does and gazelles (*ayyaloth, sebaoth*) sound much like the name of the Lord of hosts (*Elohei Sebaoth*). The poem contains a number of such plays on words which are lost in translation, but would not have been lost to the original hearers.

The daughters of Jerusalem are charged not to "awaken love." Once again there are several suggestions as to the meaning. Some commentators suggest that the lovers simply do not want to be disturbed. They wish to be left to themselves until they are ready to be interrupted. But the passage is not speaking directly of the lovers. It talks of love. The idea, then, is that you can't hurry love. Sometimes people are so eager to find love that they rush into an unwise relationship. On the religious level, in their desire for inner peace and God's love, people often grasp at something less than the real thing. But real love in marriage and in our spiritual life is a gift from God. We can't force it or hurry it. Give it time. Give God time. He can bless your marriage and your life with love. Meanwhile, stay close to him and his Word, the only source for real, lasting love.

⁸Listen! My lover!
  Look! Here he comes,
leaping across the mountains,
  bounding over the hills.
⁹My lover is like a gazelle or a young stag.
  Look! There he stands behind our wall,
gazing through the windows,
  peering through the lattice.
¹⁰My lover spoke and said to me,
  "Arise, my darling,
  my beautiful one, and come with me.
¹¹See! The winter is past;
  the rains are over and gone.
¹²Flowers appear on the earth;
  the season of singing has come,
the cooing of doves
  is heard in our land.
¹³The fig tree forms its early fruit;
  the blossoming vines spread their fragrance.
Arise, come, my darling;
  my beautiful one, come with me."

These verses mark another change in scenery. From the banquet hall we move back to the countryside. "Listen! My lover!" is literally, "The voice of my lover!" She hears his voice and is thrilled.

Throughout the poem she refers to Solomon as her "lover." This is not to imply the idea, often connected with the word "lover" today, of an illicit sexual relationship. She uses it simply as a term of endearment for the one she loves. Not until the marriage scene (3:6—5:1) does the Song speak of the physical consummation of that love. It is interesting that Solomon's other name, Jedidiah (2 Samuel 12:25), means "loved by the Lord."

Solomon's excitement is as great as hers. He is pictured as bounding across the country side to reach his beloved. The poem likens Solomon to a gazelle or young stag. These animals symbolize youthful vigor and speed. In 2 Samuel 2:18 a swift young man is described as "fleet-footed as a wild gazelle," and in Psalm 18:33 David exalts in God's protection, "He makes my feet like the feet of a deer."

Having hurried to his beloved's house, the king eagerly peers through the windows for a glimpse of her. In verses 10-13 the beloved quotes from Solomon. He invites her to come outdoors. Palestine's rainy winter season — roughly November to March — is past. As he invites his beloved to join him, Solomon paints a beautiful word-picture of spring: flowers, doves cooing, trees and vines blossoming and filling the air with fragrance, the whole earth alive with song.

Next to the olive tree, the fig tree was the most important tree in Israel. It is frequently mentioned in Scripture. This tree blossoms in March and soon produces its "early fruit." The actual figs come later and are not ripe until fall.

The picture of springtime is another one that Scripture applies to Christ and his people, the church: "Israel will bud and blossom and fill all the world with fruit" (Isaiah 27:6). When Christ came, he made everything new and fresh. To this day his gospel produces life and fruit wherever it is sown.

The unknown author of the hymn "Beautiful Savior" may well have been thinking of Solomon's Song when he wrote these lines:

Fair are the meadows,
Fair are the woodlands,
Robed in flowers of blooming spring;
Jesus is fairer,
Jesus is purer;
He makes our sorrowing spirit sing.

162

Lover

¹⁴My dove in the clefts of the rock,
  in the hiding places on the mountainside,
show me your face,
  let me hear your voice;
for your voice is sweet,
  and your face is lovely.
¹⁵Catch for us the foxes,
  the little foxes
that ruin the vineyards,
  our vineyards that are in bloom.

Beloved

¹⁶My lover is mine and I am his;
  he browses among the lilies.
¹⁷Until the day breaks
  and the shadows flee,
turn, my lover,
  and be like a gazelle
or like a young stag
  on the rugged hills.

Verse 14 is one of many places where Solomon refers to his beloved with the word "dove" (also 1:15; 4:1; 5:2; 6:9). There are several Hebrew words for dove; the one used in these verses is the dove of the rocks (*yonah*, from which the name Jonah comes). Earlier in this chapter (2:12) it was the turtledove. The NIV does not distinguish the various types but simply translates "dove" in all cases.

Like the shy rock dove who hides in the clefts of a rock, the girl remains in her house. The lover wants to see her lovely face and hear her sweet voice. This time he urges her not with talk of springtime and the great outdoors, but with a challenge they face. They must catch the foxes (or jackals) "that ruin the vineyards." Foxes get into the vineyards and destroy the crop, more by digging at the roots of the vines than by eating the grapes.

These foxes might represent anything that would destroy the love between the man and the woman. Pride, selfishness, jealousy, lust, bad habits and lack of trust are all "foxes" in a relationship. The lover rightly calls on the maiden to work at whatever problems face them. The springtime of love —before marriage — is the best time to face and overcome obstacles to love.

She responds with a statement of devotion. "My lover is mine and I am his." These words are often used as a theme for weddings, because they serve as a reminder of the faithfulness God looks for in marriage. The shepherd-king who feeds his flocks "among the lilies" and his beloved belong exclusively to each other.

In the Old Testament, engagement was the first step in marriage. The commitment between a man and woman was binding even before the actual wedding ceremony, after which the bridegroom would take the bride to live with him. Unfaithfulness on the part of engaged people held the same penalty in ancient Israel as unfaithfulness on the part of those already married — death (Deuteronomy 22:22-24).

The Song's example of commitment is one our society desperately needs to learn from. Properly understood, engagement is a promise to marry. But too often engagement (like marriage itself) is treated lightly, easily entered and easily broken.

In the final verse the young woman seems to look ahead to their actual marriage. She longs for his speedy return — "like a gazelle." Life will be dark for her, until he comes and refreshes her as a morning breeze.

The last line of this section reminds us of the difficulty of the Song. Although one of the shortest books of the Bible, the Song of Songs contains the most *hapax legomena*, i.e., words which occur only once in the original language. When there is little or no opportunity to compare a word to its use in various contexts, its meaning may be uncertain. Even though it is used elsewhere in the Old Testament, the word translated "rugged" is one of the Song's many difficult words. It could also mean "separation" or "cleavage." Following this line of thought some commentators see the "hills of separation" as a reference to the woman's breasts. The verse then expresses a desire on her part for the consummation of the marriage. Other tranlations, such as the King James, treat the word as a proper noun, "the hills of Bether." Like the NIV's "rugged hills," the reference then is to obstacles; the lover should hurry over whatever obstacles lie between him and his beloved.

In either case, the maiden clearly longs for the return of Solomon. The next verses demonstrate just how much.

3 All night long on my bed
    I looked for the one my heart loves;
    I looked for him but did not find him.
²I will get up now and go about the city,
    through its streets and squares;
    I will search for the one my heart loves.
    So I looked for him but did not find him.
³The watchmen found me
    as they made their rounds in the city.
    "Have you seen the one my heart loves?"
⁴Scarcely had I passed them
    when I found the one my heart loves.
I held him and would not let him go
    till I had brought him to my mother's house,
    to the room of the one who conceived me.
⁵Daughters of Jerusalem, I charge you
    by the gazelles and by the does of the field:
Do not arouse or awaken love
    until it so desires.

Since this sequence takes place at night and on her bed, the entire passage could well be a dream. The beloved is afraid that something will happen and she will lose him before the wedding.

The Bible often pictures night as a time of trouble. In his suffering Job describes the sorrows of the night: "Nights of misery have been assigned to me. When I lie down I think, 'How long before I get up?' The night drags on, and I toss till dawn" (Job 7:3). Only in heaven will we be entirely free from the darkness and sorrows of the night (Revelation 22:5).

In her night of misery the beloved searches but fails to find her lover. Four times she speaks of him as "the one my heart [literally, soul] loves," indicating her deep attachment to him.

She goes into the streets in search of him. Whether she is dreaming this or actually walking in the streets is immaterial. Women were not to go out alone at night. This, therefore, is a picture of her agitated state of mind.

At first she doesn't find her lover, but the city watchmen find her. Later (5:7) she will have another, more tragic encounter with some evil watchmen. At times the prophets described preachers and spiritual leaders as watchmen. For example, God said to Ezekiel, "I have made you a watchman for the house of Israel; so hear the word I speak and give them warning from me" (Ezekiel 3:17). Spiritual watchmen are to point out dangers as well as direct people to Christ.

The beloved asks the watchmen whether they have seen "the one my heart loves." It seems they gave her good directions, for as soon as she leaves them, she finds the object of her search. She clings to him and brings him to her house. Soon she will be able to stay with him forever. Their wedding is fast approaching.

The first major part of the Song of Songs ends with the refrain, "Do not arouse or awaken love. . . . " It brings a reassuring conclusion to the beloved's frantic search for her lover. Though she feared she had lost him, he was never far from her. It was only a matter of time and she would see him again.

Before we move into the next division, The Wedding, a summary of this first part is in order. We have looked at various approaches to the Song and have seen two main streams running through the poem — the blossoming of love between a man and a woman and, behind that, a picture of the love between Christ and his people. The first is a beautiful story of love in the springtime. Marked by openness, forgiveness and purity, such love is truly a gift from God. Christian young people will pray that they may find and give this kind of love in their own marriages.

The second love is also a gift from God. Christ's forgiving love for us is always fresh and pure. Though in the night of sorrow we may feel we have lost him, he is never far away from us.

*"Come with me from Lebanon, my bride,
come with me from Lebanon."*

THE WEDDING
SONG OF SONGS 3:6—5:1

The hot summer air is filled with excitement as the grand procession appears on the horizon. A cry rings out, "Look! The bridegroom is coming!"

> [6]Who is this coming up from the desert
>   like a column of smoke,
> perfumed with myrrh and incense
>   made from all the spices of the merchant?
> [7]Look! It is Solomon's carriage,
>   escorted by sixty warriors,
>   the noblest of Israel,
> [8]all of them wearing the sword,
>   all experienced in battle,
> each with his sword at his side,
>   prepared for the terrors of the night.
> [9]King Solomon made for himself the carriage;
>   he made it of wood from Lebanon.
> [10]Its posts he made of silver,
>   its base of gold.
> Its seat was upholstered with purple,
>   its interior lovingly inlaid
>   by the daughters of Jerusalem.
> [11]Come out, you daughters of Zion,
>   and look at King Solomon wearing the crown,
>   the crown with which his mother crowned him
> on the day of his wedding,
>   the day his heart rejoiced.

This is one of a number of Scripture passages which describe the ancient Jewish wedding procession. Psalm 45 depicts the pageantry of a royal marriage, and Jesus' parable of the ten virgins (Matthew 25:1-13) captures the anticipation of a late-night procession. In his book *Manners and Customs of Bible Lands*, Fred Wight gives some insight into this custom:

Sometimes the bride's relations would conduct her from her father's house to the house of her finance, where her new home was to be. But more often, as was the case of the ten virgins in Christ's parable, the bridegroom himself went in person to bring her to his home for the wedding festivities to take place there. . . .

The bridegroom set out with the bride from the house of her parents, and there followed a grand procession all the way to his house. The streets of Asiatic cities were dark, and it was necessary that anybody venturing forth at night should carry a lamp or torch. Those invited guests, who did not go to the bride's home were allowed to join the procession along the way, and go with the whole group to the marriage feast. Without a torch or lamp they couldn't join the procession, or enter the bridegroom's house. . . .

In going from the bride's house to the groom's house, the bride allowed her hair to be loose and flowing [to be arranged by women at the groom's house], and she had her face veiled. Some of her own relations preceded her in the procession, and scattered ears of parched grain to the children along the way. There were demonstrations of joy all along the road to the destination. Part of the procession included men who played on drums or other musical instruments. And there was dancing along the way. . . . [6]

The Song pictures Solomon coming to take his bride. He is "coming up from the desert." Since the time of the Exodus the desert or wilderness came to symbolize the transition from bondage to freedom, from humiliation to glory. Here it symbolizes the king's transition from his former state to the joys of marriage. He is surrounded by a wealth of colors and scents, as a smell of incense mixes with the dust swirling up from the road to form a fragrant cloud.

In describing this royal procession the poet gives special attention first to Solomon's escort and then to his carriage. According to 1 Samuel 27:2 and 30:9, King David had 600 personal troops. The sixty warriors accompanying Solomon might then be the elite, the tenth part of the royal bodyguard. This elite group consisted of experienced warriors, the cream of the crop.

At a spiritual level these armed warriors represent the angels who will accompany Christ as he returns in glory at the end of the world (Matthew 25:31). Indeed, Jesus depicts his glorious return as that of a bridegroom coming to take his bride home. "And if I go and prepare a place for you, I will come back and take you to be with me that you also may be where I am" (John 14:3).

Solomon's carriage is also splendid. The words translated "carriage" most likely refer to a palanquin, or couch, carried by servants. It was custom-made of rare and expensive materials — gold, silver and wood from Lebanon. Purple was the color of royalty; it was extracted from Mediterranean shellfish. The New Testament relates how the soldiers put a purple robe on Jesus as a way of mocking "the king of the Jews" (John 19:2,3). Little did they realize the color truly befit the King of kings! The inside of Solomon's elaborate palanquin or carriage was "lovingly inlaid" by the women of Jerusalem, also known as Zion.

Now these women are invited to come and see the great king in procession. The final verse of this passage turns our attention from everything around Solomon to the man himself. He wears a wedding crown with which his mother Bathsheba crowned him. This crowning was different from the royal coronation in which the high priest crowned the king (cf. 1 Kings 1:32-48; 2 Kings 11:11-20). According to ancient custom, not only the king but every bridegroom wore a crown. Fred Wight offers a description of the ancient groom:

> When the night arrived for the wedding festivities to begin, and it was time to go for the bride, the groom was dressed as much like a king as possible. If he were rich enough to afford it, he wore a gold crown. Otherwise it would be a garland of fresh flowers. His garments would be scented with frankincense and myrrh, his girdle would be a silken one brilliantly colored, his sandals would be figured and carefully laced, and all of this would give effect to the flowing drapery of the loose robes and to the graceful bearing peculiar to the lands of the East. For the time, the peasant seemed a prince among his fellows, and all paid him the deference due to exalted rank.[7]

Just as every groom became a king on his wedding day, so for a day Solomon becomes something other than the king. On his wedding day he is everyman who experiences the joy of love. This is "the day his heart rejoiced."

Lover

4
> How beautiful you are, my darling!
> Oh, how beautiful!
> Your eyes behind your veil are doves.
> Your hair is like a flock of goats
> descending from Mount Gilead.

²Your teeth are like a flock of sheep just shorn,
  coming up from the washing.
Each has its twin;
  not one of them is alone.
³Your lips are like a scarlet ribbon;
  your mouth is lovely.
Your temples behind your veil
  are like the halves of a pomegranate.
⁴Your neck is like the tower of David,
  built with elegance;
on it hang a thousand shields,
  all of them shields of warriors.
⁵Your two breasts are like two fawns,
  like twin fawns of a gazelle
  that browse among the lilies.
⁶Until the day breaks
  and the shadows flee,
I will go to the mountain of myrrh
  and to the hill of incense.
⁷All beautiful you are, my darling;
  there is no flaw in you.

The description of the bridegroom is complete. With these verses we turn to the bride. Wight notes that "the adorning of the bride was a very costly and elaborate affair. Much time was given to the preparation of her person."⁸ As Solomon beholds his bride he extols her beauty. He begins by describing seven of her features. It is no accident that he chooses seven. It is the number of completion and perfection. (See the comments on Ecclesiastes 3:1-8.) In the king's eyes his bride is perfect.

First he speaks of her eyes. Again he calls them doves, as he watches them flutter from behind her veil. Normally women did not wear veils, as was noted in the comments on

1:7. On special occasions, however, they would veil their faces. When Rebekah was first presented to her future husband Isaac "she took her veil and covered herself" (Genesis 24:65). And when Jacob received Leah as his wife he didn't recognize her; apparently she was veiled (Genesis 29:22-25). It seems that engagements and weddings were two occasions for wearing the veil.

The second feature Solomon describes is her hair. The comparison with a "flock of goats" may strike us as somewhat strange. But if you've ever seen a flock of black goats moving down a hillside, you'll understand the imagery of her long, graceful, jet-black hair flowing in the wind. Gilead is a mountain to the east of the Sea of Galilee. It is one of many references to the bride's northern origins. Solomon shows his consideration for his bride with numerous favorable allusions to the land she loves.

Thirdly, the king speaks of her teeth. They are white and smooth and glistening, like newly shorn sheep coming up out of the water. The mention of twins pictures the evenness of her teeth.

Her lips and mouth are mentioned next. The lips "like a scarlet ribbon" may be a reference to lipstick, since cosmetics were commonly used in the ancient Middle East. In addition to having just the right color, her mouth is perfectly formed. It is "lovely."

Solomon's fifth comparison is between her temples (or cheeks) and the pomegranate. The reddish color of this fruit would be a fitting description of her complexion. The pomegranate fruit is very refreshing and was a popular food in Bible times. Images of pomegranates ornamented the hem of the high priest's robe (Exodus 28:33) and the great pillars in front of Solomon's temple (1 Kings 7:20).

The bride's sixth feature is her neck. Here Solomon shifts from pastoral comparisons to something from his own background. Her neck is straight and noble "like the tower of David." In his palace King Solomon had hung two hundred large gold shields and three hundred small ones (1 Kings 10:16,17). The gold jewelry around her neck is reminiscent of these shields.

The seventh and last feature which Solomon praises is her breasts. While Christian readers today may be a bit squeamish about such physical references, the ancients were not. Speaking through the Prophet Isaiah, the Lord himself used this kind of language, "For you [my people] will nurse and be satisfied at her comforting breasts; you will drink deeply and delight in her overflowing abundance" (Isaiah 66:11). And Christians are urged, "Like newborn babes, crave pure spiritual milk" (1 Peter 2:2). The comparison of the woman's breasts to fawns probably depicts their softness. With this reference Solomon completes his sevenfold description of his bride's beauty.

The first part of verse 6 is a repetition of 2:17, "Until the day breaks and the shadows flee." There the woman had spoken; now Solomon uses her words. He looks forward to being with her until the break of day. With his mention of myrrh and incense he recalls her talk of perfumes and fragrances (1:12-14). The mountain of myrrh could also be a subtle allusion to Mt. Moriah on which the temple stood. The Hebrew word for myrrh, *mor*, is similar to Moriah. Certainly the best place to begin a marriage is in the presence of the Lord with his blessings and guidance!

Solomon ends his description of his bride as he began: "All beautiful you are, my darling." But now he adds, "There is no flaw in you." To him she is perfect. He sees her through the eyes of love.

In Ephesians 5:22-33 the Apostle Paul masterfully compares Christian marriage with the spiritual wedding of Christ to his people. The giving and forgiving love a hus-

band should have for his wife is a picture of Christ's love for
his church.

"Husbands, love your wives, just as Christ loved the
church and gave himself up for her." Christ has died for us
and has cleansed us from our sins. In God's sight we are
perfect; he views us through the eyes of love. In this same
way, husbands are to love their wives.

> **8Come with me from Lebanon, my bride,**
> **come with me from Lebanon.**
> **Descend from the crest of Amana,**
> **from the top of Senir, the summit of Hermon,**
> **from the lions' dens**
> **and the mountain haunts of the leopards.**
> **9You have stolen my heart, my sister, my bride;**
> **you have stolen my heart**
> **with one glance of your eyes,**
> **with one jewel of your necklace.**
> **10How delightful is your love, my sister, my bride!**
> **How much more pleasing is your love than wine,**
> **and the fragrance of your perfume than any spice!**
> **11Your lips drop sweetness as the honeycomb, my bride;**
> **milk and honey are under your tongue.**
> **The fragrance of your garments is like that of Lebanon.**

The royal wedding procession has arrived (3:6-11). Upon
seeing his bride, Solomon has praised her beauty (4:1-7). He
now formally invites her to come and live with him (4:8-11).
As he asks her to leave her northern home and accompany
him to his palace in Jerusalem, the king reassures his bride
of his deep love for her.

For the first time Solomon calls his beloved "my bride."
His invitation to leave her homeland makes mention of
several mountains or mountain ranges — Lebanon, Amana
and Hermon. All of these lie to the north of Galilee, and

Solomon uses them in a general way to refer to the north country. Each of these names has connections with Bible history.

The name Lebanon means "white" and comes from the area's impressive snowcapped mountain range which runs parallel to the Mediterranean coast. This area is still famous for the cedar trees which were used in the construction of Solomon's temple (1 Kings 5:6). The little country of Lebanon is probably the most beautiful part of the Middle East; it is tragic that in our day this land has experienced so much warfare and destruction.

A few miles to the east of the Lebanon mountains lies a parallel range known as the Anti-Lebanon range. The highest peak is Mt. Hermon (9,232 feet), also called Senir, located about forty miles northeast of the Sea of Galilee. Mt. Hermon's melting snows are a main source of the Jordan River. In the midst of an arid land, "the dew of Hermon" (Psalm 133:3) came to symbolize life and joy. Many consider this the site of Christ's transfiguration.

The other mountainous area mentioned by Solomon is Amana. These mountains lie at the northern end of the Anti-Lebanon range. From them come the waters of the Abana River, which flows through the city of Damascus. When the Prophet Elisha told Naaman to wash in the Jordan River and be cleansed of his leprosy, Naaman, who was from Damascus, at first replied, "Are not Abana and Pharpar, the rivers of Damascus, better than any of the waters of Israel?" (2 Kings 5:12) The northern heights with their forests and sparkling rivers were known for their beauty.

But Solomon reminds his bride that he is also removing her from the dangers of that region, "the lions' dens and the mountain haunts of the leopards." These animals once abounded in the Bible lands and were a very real danger in the countryside. (Leopards are still to be found in the region.) Samson was once attacked by a lion (Judges 14:5,6), and David had to kill a lion in order to protect his flock of sheep (1 Samuel 17:34-36). The Old Testament also uses these animals in a symbolic way to represent dangers and punishments. Through the Prophet Jeremiah God warned his people, "A lion from the forest will attack them, . . . a leopard will lie in wait near their towns to tear to pieces any who venture out" (Jeremiah 5:6). As Solomon protects his wife in the Song, Christ protects his people from evil. Likewise husbands ought to care for their wives.

In reassuring his bride of his care and love, Solomon calls to mind how she has stolen his heart. A second time he calls her "my bride" while also referring to her as "my sister"! This is a term of endearment and has no incestuous connotation. It expresses a desire for familiarity.

Solomon picks up on some of the things his beloved had said during the days of their courtship. It's as if he recalls every word she's ever uttered. The king declares that her love is more pleasing "than wine"; earlier she had exclaimed, "Your love is more delightful than wine" (1:2). Solomon now praises "the fragrance of your perfume," just as she had once said, "Pleasing is the fragrance of your perfumes" (1:3). "Your lips drop sweetness," he exclaims, even as she had opened the Song with the words, "Let him kiss me . . . " (1:2).

The king speaks of the sweetness of her kiss as "milk and honey." Surely he must also have in mind the well-known reference to the land of Israel as "the land flowing with milk and honey" (Deuteronomy 31:20). As God had blessed the people with the promised land, so Solomon's wife is a gift from the Lord. Too often married people forget that their spouse is a blessing from the Lord. Instead of begin grateful and appreciating their partner's good qualities, they find fault and complain. But the fact remains that thoughtful Christians consider their spouses as God-given gifts. For that is what they are.

Solomon's closing remark likens the fragrance of his bride's garments to that of Lebanon, perhaps a reference to the smell of cedar. That other great wedding song of the Old Testament, Psalm 45, speaks of the scent of the groom's robes, "fragrant with myrrh and aloes and cassia." Part of the richness of Solomon's Song lies in its many appeals to the five senses.

> [12]You are a garden locked up, my sister, my bride;
>   you are a spring enclosed, a sealed fountain.
> [13]Your plants are an orchard of pomegranates
>   with choice fruits,
>   with henna and nard,
> [14]nard and saffron,
>   calamus and cinnamon,
>   with every kind of incense tree,
>   with myrrh and aloes
>   and all the finest spices.
> [15]You are a garden fountain,
>   a well of flowing water
>   streaming down from Lebanon.

The wedding procession and the rejoicing have ended. From this point on until the end of the wedding section the imagery shifts to that of a garden. With this shy scene begins the consummation of love (4:12-5:1).

Solomon says, "You are a garden locked up." The enclosed, walled garden is still common in the Middle East. It keeps out thieves and animals; only the rightful owner has access to it. That the bride is a closed garden indicates that she is a virgin. She has kept herself pure for her husband. The groom emphasizes this thought by adding that she is also "a spring enclosed, a sealed fountain." This ideal is what the Bible holds up for young Christians. In our age of premarital sexual promiscuity it is still God's plan that a couple keep themselves only for their marriage partner.

Under the Old Testament laws a young woman would be stoned to death for "being promiscuous while still in her father's house," that is, before she married and left. And married partners who were unfaithful met with the same fate. (See Deuteronomy 22:13-29.) Such is the high value God has placed on purity and total commitment between husband and wife.

Even though we do not live under the same civil laws, we also are to conduct ourselves in chastity before and after marriage. The New Testament points this out in numerous places. For instance, Hebrews 13:4 asserts, "Marriage should be honored by all, and the marriage bed kept pure, for God will judge the adulterer and all the sexually immoral." And in 1 Corinthians 6:18-20 St. Paul states, "Flee from sexual immorality. All other sins a man commits are outside his body, but he who sins sexually sins against his own body. Do you not know that your body is a temple of the Holy Spirit, who is in you, whom you have received from God? You are not your own; you were bought at a price. Therefore honor God with your body." If we have not kept ourselves pure, it is time to repent and change. God designed marriage to be a commitment to one's partner and no one else.

Solomon continues with a description of his bride, his garden. The word translated "orchard" is the word *pardes*, from which our word "paradise" comes. It occurs only two other places in the Old Testament — in Ecclesiastes 2:5, where it is translated as "parks," and in Nehemiah 2:8, where it is translated as "forest." The king's beloved is a paradise to him, filled with every kind of fruit and spice. We have already discussed a number of these plants: the pomegranate (4:3), henna (1:14), nard (1:12) and myrrh (1:13).

Here we can also take a brief look at the other spices and fragrances which Solomon mentions. *Saffron* is mentioned nowhere else in the entire Old Testament; a single ounce of this precious spice requires over 4,000 blossoms. *Calamus* could refer to a reed or, more likely here, to a grass from which ginger-oil is extracted. *Cinnamon* comes from the bark of a tree native to southeast Asia; it was used in the special anointing oil prepared by Moses (Exodus 30:22-29). *Incense* was the resin from another tree foreign to Israel; it was one of the wise men's gifts to Jesus (Matthew 2:11). *Aloes* could be one of several plants; quite possibly it is the same spice with which Jesus' body was buried (John 19:39,40). Solomon's naming of these rare plants shows how precious his bride is to him.

Finally, she is "a garden fountain, a well of flowing [literally, 'living'] water." She overflows with life and joy. It is interesting that Jesus describes believers in the same manner, "Whoever believes in me, as the Scripture has said, streams of living water will flow from within him" (John 7:38). While it is not certain just what Scripture passage he is referring to (cf. Isaiah 58:11; Zechariah 14:8), Christ's words reflect those of the Song. As the bride of Christ, believers are filled with the water of eternal life.

To underscore what was said in our Introduction, when we see spiritual references in the Song, it is not because we are reading something into it. Rather, we find ourselves viewing marriage as the Bible itself does throughout its pages. The marriage relationship is a constant reminder of that other, eternal relationship between Jesus and his bride, the church.

Beloved
> [16]Awake, north wind,
> and come, south wind!

> Blow on my garden,
>> that its fragrance may spread abroad.
> Let my lover come into his garden
>> and taste its choice fruits.

Lover

5 I have come into my garden, my sister, my bride;
I have gathered my myrrh with my spice.
I have eaten my honeycomb and my honey;
I have drunk my wine and my milk.

The beloved takes up the picture of the closed garden, as she opens it to her husband on their wedding. She invites the winds to "blow on my garden." The right blend of the cool north wind from the mountains with the warm south wind from the desert creates a good climate for producing crops. The bride's wish is that she might be for her husband that beautiful garden he has described. Now is the time for love's fullest awakening.

She lovingly submits to her husband's desire. This, too, is in keeping with marriage as outlined in Ephesians 5:22-33. The husband is to love his wife with a Christlike love; she is to "submit to" and "respect" her husband. "As the church submits to Christ, so also wives should submit to their husbands in everything," states St. Paul.

These are the roles God has assigned in marriage. It is not a relationship of tyrant and menial slave, as some disparagingly say. No, it is a bond of loving and giving, modeled after the tie between God and his people. Just as the spiritual bond has a head, so does the marriage bond. The Ephesians passage points out, "For the husband is the head of the wife as Christ is the head of the church."

In the union between husband and wife there is another important factor which the bride touches on with the words, "Let my lover come into his garden." We belong above all to

God our Creator and Savior. In marriage we also belong to our spouse. The bride's garden is "his garden," too. The Apostle Paul underscores this truth as well. "The wife's body does not belong to her alone but also to her husband. In the same way, the husband's body does not belong to him alone but also to his wife" (1 Corinthians 7:4).

Following the consummation of their marriage, the groom exults, "I have come into my garden. . . . " He has entered the garden, which belongs to him and to no other man. The myrrh and spices, the wine and milk and honey are his to enjoy.

With this garden scene the Song of Songs harks back to the Garden of Eden and the first couple (Genesis 2:18-25). When God created the woman and brought her to man, Adam exclaimed with joy, "This is now bone of my bones and flesh of my flesh." The Genesis account continues, " . . . . they will become one flesh. The man and his wife were both naked, and they felt no shame."

Since the fall into sin, God's institution of marriage has been ravaged by every kind of abuse and wickedness. Yet, at its best, married life can still be a taste of Eden. This happens when husband and wife live together under God and follow his will for their lives. It takes more than romantic love or physical attraction to make a union in which two people truly become one flesh. It takes God.

He designed marriage. He wants it to be a happy experience. The Song's final words on the wedding show this:

Friends

> **Eat, O friends, and drink;**
> **drink your fill, O lovers.**

Together with the bride's words (4:16) and the groom's (5:1), this half-verse falls in the middle of the poem. This center section is the heart of the Song. The bride and groom have given themselves to each other. The two have become one. Everything in the courtship and wedding led up to that point. Everything that now follows reaffirms it.

According to the NIV these two lines are spoken by the "Friends." Yet since the poem has just treated the most intimate portion of the wedding, its consummation, it's unlikely that the friends would be present. Other have suggested that the wind is personified and speaking to the lovers in their garden. There is a better choice of speakers — God himself. It seems fitting that the Lord would seal this wedding with his blessings. The uniting of a man and woman in marriage has God's blessings. One of Solomon's proverbs says it this way: "He who finds a wife finds what is good and receives favor from the Lord" (Proverbs 18:22).

The two are called "friends" and "lovers." In these roles husband and wife fulfill God's original plan for marriage (Genesis 2:18-25). In the beginning God said, "It is not good for the man to be alone. I will make a helper suitable for him." To answer the man's need for companionship God created woman. God designed marriage to be the closest friendship between two human beings. Moreover, the Genesis account also declares that "they will become one flesh." They become one in many ways, but especially physically, sexually. This is why sexual unfaithfulness strikes so devastating a blow against the marriage union. In the same context in which he speaks of our bodies as the temple of God, the Apostle Paul treats this topic, "Shall I then take the members of Christ and unite them with a prostitute? Never! Do you not know that he who unites himself with a prostitute is one with her in body? For it is said, 'The two will become one flesh' " (1 Corinthians 6:15,16). Sex is meant for marriage.

Friendship and sexual unity are two of marriage's chief blessings. So the two friends and lovers are urged to eat and drink their fill. God smiles on the couple and wishes them the joys of married life.

With this benediction the Song's wedding comes to a close. It would be wrong for us to leave this happy scene without one more look at our heavenly bridegroom Jesus Christ. At the end of the world he will come in glory with all his angels and take his bride to be with him. Then we shall join in "the wedding supper of the Lamb" (Revelation 19:7-9). But even now we have the joy of his unseen presence. Likening himself to the best man and Christ to the groom, John the Baptist expressed the joy of every believer when he said, "The bride belongs to the bridegroom. The friend who attends the bridegroom waits and listens for him, and is full of joy when he hears the bridegroom's voice. The joy is mine, and it is now complete" (John 3:29). Christ himself also spoke of the joy he brings, "How can the guests of the bridegroom mourn while he is with them?" (Matthew 9:15)

The Bible makes many such comparisons between a wedding and our spiritual bond with Christ. Scripture also notes some differences. The husband-wife bond lasts only for this life and ends with death (Matthew 22:30; Romans 7:2); with Christ we have eternal life (John 11:25,26). Earthly marriage is consummated with the physical union; "but he who unites himself with the Lord is one with him in spirit" (1 Corinthians 6:17). Finally, Christ's dealings with us are always perfect; our dealings with one another are frequently distorted by sin.

This last point leads us into the next part of the Song of Songs. There for the first time a problem arises between the loving couple.

"Open to me, my sister, my darling."

SEPARATION AND REUNION
SONG OF SONGS 5:2—8:4

It is cold and damp outside. The lover wants to come inside and be with his beloved, to stay with her till midnight and beyond. But her response is slow and cold.

Beloved

> 2I slept but my heart was awake.
> Listen! My lover is knocking:
> "Open to me, my sister, my darling,
>   my dove, my flawless one.
> My head is drenched with dew,
>   my hair with the dampness of the night."
> 3I have taken off my robe —
>   must I put it on again?
> I have washed my feet —
>   must I soil them again?

The honeymoon is over. Now we find the couple in a different setting as the anticipation and excitement of their courtship and wedding pass into the routine of day-to-day life. The wife is alone; no doubt she has her own room in the palace. Her husband has been away and has now returned.

The beloved is either half-awake or dreaming, as she indicates with the words, "I slept but my heart was awake." A sudden knocking at the door interrupts her drowsy state. It is her husband. His feelings are evident from the many terms of affection with which he urges her to open the door — "my sister, my darling, my dove, my flawless one." Nowhere else in the poem does Solomon address his beloved with so long a list of endearing words.

But she is unwilling. It's too much bother. What a contrast we find between her indifference here and that night before their wedding when she couldn't sleep for thoughts of "the one my heart loves"! (3:1)

Although the circumstances might vary greatly, this scene has been reenacted countless times in countless marriages. Married life is full of little incidents in which one or both spouses fail to respond to the needs and desires of the other. Bit by bit walls of hurt and bitterness begin to separate husband and wife. "Incompatibility" is the term often used as a catchall to describe the end result.

While the Song does not mention divorce, its third major section opens on the all-too-common note of marital discord. One commentator observes, "Actually she was no different from many a modern housewife who becomes so involved in taking care of her husband's children and house that she forgets about her husband."[9] Wives, of course, don't have a monopoly on indifference. Husbands exhibit the same trait as they put more time and effort into making money than into making a happy marriage.

What holds true in marriage, often is the case in our spiritual lives, too. As a matter of fact, marriage problems are often related to spiritual problems. When there is something wrong in one area, the other will also suffer. We can appreciate this all the more as we understand how the marriage relationship is patterned on the spiritual. Jesus says, "I stand at the door and knock. If anyone hears my voice and opens the door, I will go in and eat with him, and he with me" (Revelation 3:20). Too often we respond with selfish and sleepy indifference. We don't want to be bothered. In this way our life with God begins to break down.

⁴My lover thrust his hand through the latch-opening;
  my heart began to pound for him.
⁵I arose to open for my lover,
  and my hands dripped with myrrh,
 my fingers with flowing myrrh,
  on the handles of the lock.
⁶I opened for my lover,
  but my lover had left; he was gone.
  My heart had gone out to him when he spoke.
 I looked for him but did not find him.
 I called him but he did not answer.

The beloved continues relating her story. The lover stopped knocking and reached his hand through an opening in the door. At this, she exclaims, "My heart began to pound for him." And so she went to open the door for him.

The mention of her hands dripping with myrrh seems to refer to the ancient custom of a lover leaving myrrh on the handle of his beloved's door. It may be that this reminder of his love made her want the king even more. But "my lover had left; he was gone." She looked for him and called for him in the night. He did not answer and was not to be found.

The Song doesn't say exactly why the lover left. From what follows later in this chapter, it seems he wasn't angry. Most likely he felt rejected. Again, it does not take much effort to apply this situation to marriages today. Indifference, sharp words, hurt feelings, withdrawal — one thing leads to another. If the pattern isn't broken it can lead to the destruction of a marriage. As we see them now, the lovers are separated.

Similarly Jesus warns us about rejecting him. To those who continually put Christ off and turn their backs on him, he declares, "I am going away, and you will look for me, and you will die in your sin" (John 8:21). *Now* is the time to listen to Christ, just like now is the time to work on your marriage. Tomorrow may be too late.

> ⁷**The watchmen found me**
> **as they made their rounds in the city.**
> **They beat me, they bruised me;**
> **they took away my cloak,**
> **those watchmen of the walls!**
> ⁸**O daughters of Jerusalem, I charge you —**
> **if you find my lover,**
> **what will you tell him?**
> **Tell him I am faint with love.**

Friends

> ⁹**How is your beloved better than others,**
> **most beautiful of women?**
> **How is your beloved better than others,**
> **that you charge us so?**

In the beloved's first encounter with the watchmen they were helpful (3:3). This time the watchmen take her cloak and beat her up!

Just as we were able to relate the good watchmen to faithful spiritual leaders, we can easily identify these evil watchmen as false prophets. They take from believers the "robe of righteousness" (Isaiah 61:10) which is theirs in Christ Jesus. By directing people away from Christ and to their own good works, these watchmen cause great harm.

It's true in our spiritual relationship with Christ — as in our marriages — that when we let the relationship slide, we are asking for all sorts of troubles. We lay ourselves open to numerous temptations and dangers. We become easy prey to wicked people and bad advice.

As the cliche puts it, sometimes the darkest hour is just before the dawn. Alone and hurt, the beloved desperately wants her lover back. Her choice of words is an obvious attempt to return to the way things were. She uses expressions she had employed in the springtime of their romance. Summoning what boldness she can, she directs her friends, the daughters of Jerusalem, "*I charge you* (2:7) — if you find *my lover* (1:14)... Tell him *I am faint with love* (2:5)*.*" With this last phrase she wants her husband to know she still loves him as she did before. Clearly, she has repented of her indifference.

The friends, who have probably been attending to the beloved in her misery, now comfort her. They also remind her of the former days of love. They address her as "most beautiful of women," just as they did in the beginning of the poem (1:8). To strengthen her in her resolve to amend the wrong, they ask questions which lead her to think about why her lover is so important to her. Why, they ask, are you now so eager to find him?

This is a wise approach on the part of the friends. They are getting her to reconsider her blessings. Maybe next time she will think twice before treating her husband so rudely. It's easy for all of us to become indifferent to our spouses. Rather than taking our partner for granted or concentrating on defects, we can learn from the friends. Periodically we ought to consider the God-given blessings we enjoy through our husband or wife — companionship, a home life, a lifelong partner and many other gifts.

Beloved

> [10]My lover is radiant and ruddy,
>   outstanding among ten thousand.
> [11]His head is purest gold;
>   his hair is wavy
>   and black as a raven.
> [12]His eyes are like doves
>   by the water streams,
>   washed in milk,
>   mounted like jewels.

> ¹³His cheeks are like beds of spice
>   yielding perfume.
> His lips are like lilies
>   dripping with myrrh.
> ¹⁴His arms are rods of gold
>   set with chrysolite.
> His body is like polished ivory
>   decorated with sapphires.
> ¹⁵His legs are pillars of marble
>   set on bases of pure gold.
> His appearance is like Lebanon,
>   choice as its cedars.
> ¹⁶His mouth is sweetness itself;
>   he is altogether lovely.
> This is my lover, this my friend,
>   O daughters of Jerusalem.

In answer to the friends' questions, the beloved now tells why her lover is "better than others." The beloved's description of her husband bursts with colorful images. She describes him physically, but in a manner which symbolizes inner qualities.

Before she gets into the actual description, she simply exclaims that her "radiant and ruddy" husband is "outstanding among ten thousand." The word for ruddy is the Hebrew word *adom*, from which the name Adam comes (for he was taken from the earth). The lover, then, is earth-colored, reddish-tan. We need not take the number ten thousand literally; she is using it to represent a very large number. In a word, her husband is unique.

The description of him that follows is also unique. Although ancient poems commonly described female beauty, the reverse was rare. The description begins with his head and moves down to his feet. Later (7:1-9) Solomon will describe her beauty, beginning with her feet and going up to her head.

His head is golden, referring to his radiant tan coloring. Wavy, raven-black hair adorns his head. Here we see the first of many sources the beloved will use to describe her husband's beauty. She compares his features to precious metals (gold), birds (ravens, doves), jewels (chrysolite, sapphires), spices, myrrh, perfumes, flowers (lilies), ivory, marble, and majestic trees (cedars). While modern writers usually avoid mixing so many different comparisons in such a short space, the ancient oriental poet had no such qualms.

In describing his eyes she heaps one image on top of another: doves, by the streams, washed in milk, mounted like jewels. These pictures depict the sparkle and the white of his eyes.

Verse 13 discusses more features of Solomon's face, his cheeks and lips. Here the emphasis is on pleasant smells instead of marvelous appearance. The lips "like lilies dripping with myrrh" could refer to his pleasant manner of speaking or to his sweet kiss, which she previously mentioned (1:2).

Next she describes the king's arms. They, too, are golden. His arms are adorned with "chrysolite," a yellow or greenish gem. Although the NIV translates the word in this manner, the exact meaning is uncertain. The Hebrew says "Tarshish." A better translation might be "jewels of Tarshish" or "Spanish jewels," since Tarshish was an ancient name for Spain.

Solomon's body is "like polished ivory." It is decorated, clothed, with sapphires. The Hebrew term *sappir*, from which our English word sapphire comes, probably refers to the blue lapis lazuli which abounds in the Middle East and not to the modern sapphire stone.

Comparing his legs to marble (or alabaster), the beloved continues her description of her husband. She has used a number of terms to describe her lover's skin coloring: radiant, ruddy, golden, ivory, marble. All these varying hues are most complimentary to the object of her praise. Marble symbolizes strength as well as beauty.

In likening his overall appearance to Lebanon and its cedars, she points to his majesty, strength, beauty and priceless value.

In her final reference to his mouth, she mentions his entire mouth and not just his lips. Most likely this would include his fair speech in addition to his handsome appearance.

With this reference, incidentally, she has listed a total of ten features of Solomon. Like the number seven, ten is a popular biblical number. It signifies completeness. We think of the Ten Commandments, the tithe (a tenth given to the Lord), ten men forming a town council (Ruth 4:2).

Having poured out one magnificent word of praise after another, the beloved sums up her feelings: "he is altogether lovely." This, she says to her friends, is my lover and friend. The description has been physical. Yet it hints at other more important traits such as strength, dignity and grace.

In Revelation 1:12-16 St. John relates the glorious appearance of Christ. John describes Christ's head and hair as being "white as snow," his eyes "like blazing fire," his feet "like bronze glowing in a furnace" and his voice "like the sound of rushing waters." John adds, "His face was like the sun shining in all its brilliance." Although John's portrait of Christ differs in many details from the description of Solomon, it leaves an overall impression not unlike that of the Song. Both pictures are of glorious and radiant kings.

Friends

6
> **Where has your lover gone,**
> **most beautiful of women?**
> **Which way did your lover turn,**
> **that we may look for him with you?**

Beloved

> ²My lover has gone down to his garden,
>   to the beds of spices,
> to browse in the gardens
>   and to gather lilies.
> ³I am my lover's and my lover is mine;
>   he browses among the lilies.

Obviously the beloved loves her husband very much. The friends now ask for some clues so they can help her find him. Where did he head? Do you remember which way he turned?

Earlier she had searched for him in vain. Now it suddenly occurs to her where he might have gone. She is sure that he has gone to "his garden." No longer is she worried and desperate. As she depicts Solomon in the garden, she confidently asserts that they belong to each other.

We might picture this scene in one of two ways. Perhaps she recalls how they frequently spent time with each other in the royal garden. She is confident that he has gone there and that she will find him there. When we recall how the word garden was used in the wedding scene, we might picture this episode in another way. *She* is the garden (4:12-5:1). He has gone to "his" garden — in her renewed confidence she knows that he will be waiting for her.

In either case she is sure she has not lost her husband. Why this sudden renewal of confidence? The answer lies in her statement, "I am my lover's and my lover is mine." Back in 2:16 the beloved used the same expression (although the words were reversed). There we discussed the importance of commitment in a relationship. Knowing that she and her husband are unconditionally committed to each other, the beloved realizes that she has not lost him.

The old English word for marriage was wedlock. This word basically means "pledge," and it emphasizes what lies at the heart of the marriage union. As God designed it, marriage is based on a lifelong commitment between a man and a woman. This is a commitment to be faithful and loving, through misunderstanding and disappointments, until death. The beloved and her lover have freely and willingly consented to give themselves to each other. As she thinks of this her spirit soars. Of course he will not leave her. They belong to each other!

In Ecclesiastes 5:4-6 Solomon discussed the importance of vows. It is a good idea for couples to review their marriage vows from time to time, and then ask God's help to do their best to live by their promises.

Lover

⁴You are beautiful, my darling, as Tirzah,
   lovely as Jerusalem,
   majestic as troops with banners.
⁵Turn your eyes from me;
   they overwhelm me.
 Your hair is like a flock of goats
   descending from Gilead.
⁶Your teeth are like a flock of sheep
   coming up from the washing.
 Each has its twin,
   not one of them is alone.
⁷Your temples behind your veil
   are like the halves of a pomegranate.
⁸Sixty queens there may be,
   and eighty concubines,
   and virgins beyond number;
⁹but my dove, my perfect one, is unique,
   the only daughter of her mother,
   the favorite of the one who bore her.
 The maidens saw her and called her blessed;
   the queens and concubines praised her.

No sooner has the beloved expressed her assurance that her husband is hers, and he is by her side. Just as she has praised her lover, he now proclaims his love for her.

She had compared his appearance to the majesty of Lebanon; he also begins his praise with majestic comparisons. She is "beautiful" as Tirzah, "lovely as Jerusalem." Centuries before Solomon, Tirzah had been captured by Joshua (Joshua 12:24) and after Solomon's time it became the first capital of the northern kingdom of Israel (1 Kings 15:33). That the writer should mention Tirzah in the same breath with Jerusalem argues for the Solomonic authorship of the poem. Throughout the Song, and especially here, the poet treats the entire land as a unit. There is no hint at a division between north and south. In Solomon's day Tirzah may well have been a garden city. Obviously it was a beautiful place; the name Tirzah means "delight."

Jerusalem, of course, was the royal city. Scripture often extols the beauty of Jerusalem, "beautiful in its loftiness, the joy of the whole earth" (Psalm 48:2) and "perfect in beauty" (Psalm 50:2). The greatest joy that would come from this city would be that here the world's Savior was to culminate his work of salvation with his death and resurrection. Revelation 21:2 pictures Christ's bride, the church, as the "new Jerusalem": "I saw the Holy City, the new Jerusalem, coming down out of heaven from God, prepared as a bride beautifully dressed for her husband."

Next Solomon likens his wife to troops with banners. This is hardly a gentle description of the woman! Yet it emphasizes the hold she had on him. She came, she saw, she conquered.

Especially does she conquer him with her eyes. They simply "overwhelm" him. He wants her to look away so he can continue speaking and reassure her of his love.

If the next descriptions seem familiar, it's because Solomon has used them before. His word-pictures of her hair, teeth and temples are the same he used on their wedding day (4:1-3). Perhaps during their separation he began to reflect on that special day. Interestingly, Solomon does not again list all the qualities he extolled at their wedding. Has he grown somewhat indifferent himself? In the light of his other words of praise, that seems unlikely.

If the "sixty queens and eighty concubines" refer to King Solomon's harem, we have here an indication that the Song comes from a time early in his reign. Eventually he had seven hundred wives and three hundred concubines who turned his heart from the Lord (1 Kings 11:3,4). On the other hand, the poet does not specifically say he is speaking of Solomon's wives and concubines. The reference, then, is to women in general. No queen, concubine or virgin anywhere can compare with his beloved.

In either case, we come face to face with the fact that Solomon did not remain married to one woman throughout his life. Perhaps early in his reign he left his harem as he found a pure relationship with the woman described in the Song. For whatever reasons, this love was not to last. It is in his ungodly polygamy that King Solomon falls far short as a type of Christ. What made Solomon's marital foolishness all the worse is that it was done against the clear warning of Scripture. Deuteronomy 17:17 had declared that the king "must not take many wives, or his heart will be led astray."

At least for a time, however, Solomon saw clearly enough to describe the blessedness of a godly marriage. As he continues his praise of his beloved he mentions that she was "the only daughter of her mother, the favorite of the one who bore her." This passage literally says she was "the only one" of her mother. In view of the fact that she had brothers (1:6) our translation has "the only *daughter*." It could be she was the only child and that her brothers were stepbrothers. Again we can only speculate because of the limited information we have. But Solomon's point is clear. His wife is unique and special.

The maidens, queens and concubines also recognize this and join in the praise. G. Lloyd Carr comments on two of these various classes of women in the ancient world, *"Concubines* in ancient Israel were not mere bed partners. They were actually 'wives' . . . albeit of secondary rank, with certain protections and privileges that set them apart from those outside the wife/concubine categories. *Maidens* [were] unmarried women."[10] It is noteworthy that all the women are eager to join Solomon in praising his wife rather than jealously resenting her. This says much for the beloved's gentle, likable personality.

Friends
> 10**Who is this that appears like the dawn,**
>   **fair as the moon, bright as the sun,**
>   **majestic as the stars in procession?**

Lover
> 11**I went down to the grove of nut trees**
>   **to look at the new growth in the valley,**
>   **to see if the vines had budded**
>   **or the pomegranates were in bloom.**
> 12**Before I realized it,**
>   **my desire set me among the royal chariots**
>   **of my people.**[11]

The friends carry the king's praises even farther. They compare his wife to the dawn, the moon and the sun! Notice the progression from the lesser to the greater light. Her brightness increases. In the original Hebrew the next expression, "majestic as the stars in procession," is really the same one the lover had used earlier, "majestic as troops with banners" (6:4). Apparently the translators felt that in this context the troops with banners are the starry hosts of heaven.

For the most part, the NIV translators have done an excellent job with designating the speaker for each section. But as they freely admit, "In some instances the divisions and their captions are debatable." (See comments on 1:2.) This section is one such instance. In this writer's opinion it makes more sense to have the beloved speak verses 11 and 12. She is responding to the question, "Who is this . . . ?" The friends have asked to know some more about this wonderful woman. In her typical self-effacing manner she quickly shifts the spotlight away from herself and instead describes her encounter with her husband.

But what encounter is she describing? It's unlikely she is talking about how she and her husband have just been reconciled. At that time she was hardly interested in checking out the new spring growth. Nor does it seem she is describing the garden of her own person. Rather, she is thinking back to when she and Solomon first met.

We might picture their meeting something like this: It was springtime in the country. She had gone into the valley to look at the budding trees and vines. It just so happened at that time the king was passing by on his chariot. Perhaps he stopped beside her vineyard to rest. It was then that the great king and the country maiden were drawn to each other.

One thing led to another and, she recalls, "Before I realized it, my desire set me among the royal chariots of my people." The beloved has just finished listening to her husband's and friends' glowing praise. But she is still a country girl at heart, somewhat overawed that she should be the object of so much attention. Yet here she is, a queen who rides in the royal chariots. King Solomon was famous for his chariots (1 Kings 10:26); as a result of her love for him she now rides with him and is numbered among the royalty.

Friends

¹³**Come back, come back, O Shulammite;**
come back, come back, that we may gaze on you!

Lover

Why would you gaze on the Shulammite
as on the dance of Mahanaim?

Having said what little she is going to say about herself, the beloved turns to leave. The friends urge her to stay. They love her and want to "gaze" on her.

Here for the first time in the Song we encounter the beloved's name. Like so many other words in the poem the name Shulammite is rich in meaning. It is the feminine counterpart of Solomon. In English masculine-feminine forms of the same name commonly occur: Don and Donna, Paul and Pauline, Robert and Roberta. It is a fitting name for the beloved wife of Solomon who is so close to him.

The name Shulammite means "one who receives peace," while the name Solomon means "the peaceful one." Here we see an obvious parallel with Christ and his people. He is "the Prince of Peace" (Isaiah 9:6) who through his sacrificial death brings us peace with God.

The form of the name Shulammite indicates that it is not strictly a personal name, but more of a designation. She is *the* Shulammite. It is possible that the word Shulammite is a variation of Shunammite. This has whetted the appetite of Bible students as a suggestion concerning the identity of the beloved. If Shulammite and Shunammite are synonymous (and one ancient historian does link the two), then Solomon's beloved could have been Abishag, who took care of aged King David. 1 Kings 1:1-4 records this history:

When King David was old and well advanced in years, he could not keep warm even when they put covers over him. So his servants said to him, "Let us look for a young virgin to attend the king and take care of him. She can lie beside him so that our lord the king may keep warm."

Then they searched throughout Israel for a beautiful girl and found Abishag, a Shunammite, and brought her to the king. The girl was very beautiful; she took care of the king and waited on him, but the king had no intimate relations with her.

Shunem was a town in northern Israel. It's obvious from the Song that Solomon's beloved wife was from the north. Was Abishag the Shulammite of Solomon's Song? It's an interesting possibility. Yet some of the details might not quite fit together. For example, the Song implies that Solomon himself came upon the Shulammite, while according to 1 Kings the young Abishag was brought to King David. So Solomon may have come to know her through his father. On the other hand, it is possible that while the search was being made, Solomon himself participated in it and discovered Abishag.

Again, the precise circumstances behind Solomon's Song are veiled from us. The love and beauty it depicts are obvious.

The lover continues the poem as he asks the friends why they wish to gaze on the Shulammite "as on the dance of Mahanaim." Mahanaim was a site about fifteen miles east of the Jordan River on the Jabbok River. Here Jacob camped the night before he met his long-separated brother Esau (Genesis 32:1,2). The Old Testament mentions the place a number of other times. From Solomon's use of the name, it appears that a dance was named after it. This may have been a folk dance involving two groups of people, since the name Mahanaim means "two camps." The Shulammite is graceful and enjoyable to watch as was this dance.

King Solomon proceeds to answer his own question, "Why would you gaze on the Shulammite?" He goes on to describe his beautiful beloved:

7
How beautiful your sandaled feet,
  O prince's daughter!
Your graceful legs are like jewels,
  the work of a craftsman's hands.
²Your navel is a rounded goblet
  that never lacks blended wine.
Your waist is a mound of wheat
  encircled by lilies.
³Your breasts are like two fawns,
  twins of a gazelle.
⁴Your neck is like an ivory tower.
Your eyes are the pools of Heshbon
  by the gate of Bath Rabbim.
Your nose is like the tower of Lebanon
  looking toward Damascus.
⁵Your head crowns you like Mount Carmel.
  Your hair is like royal tapestry;
  the king is held captive by its tresses.
⁶How beautiful you are and how pleasing,
  O love, with your delights!
⁷Your stature is like that of the palm,
  and your breasts like clusters of fruit.
⁸I said, "I will climb the palm tree;
  I will take hold of its fruit."
May your breasts be like the clusters of the vine,
  the fragrance of your breath like apples,
⁹ and your mouth like the best wine.

Earlier we heard the beloved extol Solomon's beauty (5:10-16). She had praised ten of his features from his head on down. Starting with her feet and going up to her head Solomon now cites ten of his wife's features. On their wedding night he had lavished sevenfold praise upon his bride (4:1-7). Now it is tenfold, the other Hebrew number of perfection. In spite of the trials of marriage, his love is still as complete as when they were wed.

While she draws most of her descriptions of her lover from nature, Solomon draws largely from city life and man-made articles.

Like his beloved, the king emphasizes the physical. That God includes these portions in his Word demonstrates that physical attraction between a man and a woman can be God-pleasing. As a matter of fact, beauty is a gift from God the Creator. Regardless of our natural appearance, all of us should try to look our personal best, *especially* for our marriage partner. At the same time we will recognize that today's overemphasis on physical attractiveness is not scriptural. The Bible teaches that spiritual gifts are much more valuable and lasting. The book of Proverbs sets the correct balance in its famous section on "the wife of noble character." "Charm is deceptive, and beauty is fleeting; but a woman who fears the Lord is to be praised" (Proverbs 31:30).

We must read the Song of Songs in the context of the rest of Scripture. This means we can appreciate and enjoy the Song's delight in the beautiful without losing a proper perspective.

Solomon first extols his wife's sandaled feet. The graceful movement of her feet befits a "prince's daughter." Although not of noble birth, she has always been a princess by virtue of her noble character.

Secondly, he mentions her legs. They are rounded like crafted and polished jewels. In a word, she has an excellent figure. It is interesting that Solomon speaks of his wife as "the work of a craftman's hands," since she has always spoken of him in terms of natural beauty. Here again the poem readily lends itself to a spiritual understanding. God's infinite power, wisdom and love are part of his very nature. People, however, are created beings. And believers are people whom God has not only created, but also *re*created in Christ. "We are God's workmanship, created in Christ Jesus to do good works, which God prepared in advance for us to do" (Ephesians 2:10).

Thirdly, her navel "is a rounded goblet" full of "blended wine." With this picture Solomon seems to depict fullness and well-being.

Fourthly, Solomon's description of her waist suggests her tan color ("wheat") along with the woman's delicateness ("enriched by lilies").

Fifthly, he moves up to her breasts. The description here recalls the one Solomon used in 4:5.

Next comes her neck — noble, smooth and pure "like an ivory tower." Since King Solomon had built towns and fortifications in Lebanon (1 Kings 9:19), he may well have had in mind a specific tower from her home country.

In describing her eyes, the king introduces a definite geographical reference. Heshbon lay to the east of the Dead Sea, near Amman the modern capital of Jordan. The pools of Heshbon were near to the city's water supplies. The image is of clear, sparkling water in a hot, dry land. Again the picture is one of delight.

Solomon's eighth reference is to her nose. It is noble and straight. It's said that the upturned nose, once considered the American ideal of feminine beauty, has now given way to the "stronger" nose. The "new" look of the eighties seems more in line with the ancient ideal.

Her crowning feature is her head. Like Mt. Carmel rising splendidly along the northern Mediterranean coast of Israel, she holds high her beautiful head.

Finally, the king is captivated by her hair. The word translated "royal tapestry" is literally "purple." Her free-flowing black hair (4:1; 6:5) shimmers like the loose-hanging ends of the richest weaving. And like a royal robe wrapped around the king, her hair holds him captive.

As he has done before, the king again exclaims, "How beautiful you are . . . !" Then he turns to his desire for her. Verses 8 and 9 form one of the more explicit passages in the Song. Likening her stature to a tall, slender palm tree, the king expresses his desire for her. He longs to kiss and caress his wife.

Perhaps it was because of such passages that the old Jewish rabbis required that no one read the book until reaching the age of thirty. Yet even here the poem is chaste. To use the expression from Hebrews, marriage is "honored" and "the marriage bed kept pure" (Hebrews 13:4). The husband has expressed his feelings more openly and intimately then he ever did before. In doing this the Song's bridegroom sets a good example for all of us. Our marriages ought to be marked by a growth in intimacy and openness — especially in expressing our love for our spouse.

Now it is the wife's turn to respond:

Beloved
>May the wine go straight to my lover,
>   flowing gently over lips and teeth.
>10I belong to my lover,
>   and his desire is for me.
>11Come, my lover, let us go the countryside,
>   let us spend the night in the villages.
>12Let us go early to the vineyards
>   to see if the vines have budded,
> if their blossoms have opened,
>   and if the pomegranates are in bloom —
>   there I will give you my love.
>13The mandrakes send out their fragrances,
>   and at our door is every delicacy,
> both new and old,
>   that I have stored up for you, my lover.

The beloved takes up her lovers' wish that her mouth be "like the best of wine." She agrees and adds, "May the wine go straight to my lover...." He had wished for her love; she wants to fulfill his wish. That's the way it should be, for she belongs to him and his desire is for her.

In her invitation to escape to the countryside, we again see the Shulammite's love for the country. Once more she pictures the beauty of springtime out in the country.

The word translated "villages" is similar to the word for "henna bushes." Either translation captures the idea of getting away from the city and being alone. Sometimes couples become so caught up in their hectic schedules that they don't take time to get away together. Jobs, housework, the children and church activities are important. But they needn't get in the way of your marriage. It's said the biggest problem in marriages is not money, sex or incompatibility. It's neglect. God intends marriage partners to be united with one another. Take time to be together.

After spending the night together, the beloved suggests, they can get up early and spend the day in the great outdoors. She speaks of budding vineyards and of scarlet pomegranate blossoms. She has used these expressions before (6:11). There she related how she had been alone among the vines and pomegranates. This time she wants her husband to be with her. Amid the colors and scents of spring, she promises, "There I will give you my love."

Verse 13 introduces a new plant to the Song — the mandrake. This plant produces a fragrant purple flower and red fruit. The Bible's only other reference to the mandrake is in Genesis 30:14-18. In that episode Jacob's two wives, Leah and Rachel, bartered over some mandrakes. Among the ancients the mandrake was considered an aphrodisiac, hence its other name, the "love apple." The eating of this fragrant herb was also thought to promote conception. We can understand, then, why both Leah and Rachel wanted the plant. Leah wanted Jacob's love; Rachel wanted to have a child. The mandrake's associations with love were not lost on Solomon and his beloved.

The king's wife offers to share everything "old and new" with her husband. She shares what they have come to treasure, but she also desires to keep their relationship fresh. In our marriages we ought to do the same. Keep the best of the old — the memories and treasures. And look for new experiences, new ways to say, "I love you."

Notice how much healing has taken place since the beginning of this section of the Song. At first it was too much for her to open the door for her husband (5:2,3). Now "our door" is open with sharing and mutual commitment.

God can restore troubled marriages. He can do it even where there has been unfaithfulness and abuse. I've seen it happen. No doubt you have too. So if your marriage is less then perfect — and whose isn't? — don't give up. Even when there is no miraculous change, the Lord can give his people strength, courage and love to carry on.

8 If only you were to me like a brother,
who was nursed at my mother's breasts!
Then, if I found you outside,
I would kiss you,
and no one would despise me.
²I would lead you
and bring you to my mother's house —
she who has taught me.
I would give you spiced wine to drink,
the nectar of my pomegranates.
³His left arm is under my head
and his right arm embraces me.

⁴Daughters of Jerusalem, I charge you:
Do not arouse or awaken love
until it so desires.

In his commentary on the Song, S. Craig Glickman states, "Marriage is not really a single relationship. It is a composite of many relationships. Your partner is lover, friend, teacher, student, brother or sister and child all in one person. And the better the marriage the more evident is every aspect."[12]

The opening verses of chapter 8 depict Solomon and the Shulammite in several of these roles. First the wife wishes her husband were "like a brother." She wishes she had known him from childhood on. Besides, if he were her brother she could kiss him publicly. It is still true in parts of the Middle East that brothers and sisters are permitted to display more open affection than married couples. Proverbs 17:17 describes another aspect of a loving brother, his steadfastness in trouble: "A friend loves at all times, and a brother is born for adversity."

The Shulammite goes on to say how she would like to take the king home to her mother's house. This is another thought previously expressed (3:4). According to the NIV translation, the wife refers to her mother as "she who taught me." The subject of the verb, however, could also be her husband: "You would teach me." This seems to make more sense, for she is addressing him throughout these verses. She wants her husband to be her teacher.

In return she would give him wine and nectar. Although the poem contains numerous references to wine, this is the only one to spiced wine. As for the pomegranate nectar, this refreshing fruit was prized for its delicious taste. An old Persian proverb exclaims, "Eat eagerly only pomegranates, for their grains are from paradise."[13] The beloved wants nothing but the best for her husband!

In addition to being like a brother and a teacher, the husband is depicted as a lover. In another familiar phrase, the beloved speaks of her lover's embrace (also in 2:6). And once again she tells the daughters of Jerusalem not to "arouse or awaken love" (also 2:7; 3:5).

Like that of the lovers in the Song, the relationship between Christ and his people is many-sided. He is our brother (Mark 3:35; Romans 8:29) who sticks with us at all times. He is our teacher instructing us through the Bible in the way of salvation. He is our friend (John 15:14,15). And, as we've noted throughout this commentary, he is our heavenly bridegroom.

The third main part of the Song of Songs ends on a happy note. After their separation the lovers are together again and closer than ever.

This, too, is a picture of Christ and the church. Especially in Old Testament prophecy the people of God are frequently shown as an unfaithful or indifferent bride. "Does a maid forget her jewelry, a bride her wedding garments?" asks the Lord through the Prophet Jeremiah. "Yet my people have forgotten me, days without number" (Jeremiah 2:32).

Ezekiel 16 contains especially strong images of the people's unfaithfulness. God relates how he had loved Jerusalem and had made her his bride. But the people proved unfaithful. By forsaking the true God for the idols of Egypt, Philistia, Assyria and Babylonia, God's chosen nation became a "brazen prostitute" (16:30). "You adulterous wife! You prefer strangers to your own husband!" (16:32) Because of her sins God would punish her.

But like the tribulations of the lovers in the Song, God's dealings with his people do not end on the tragic note of separation. God goes on to say, "Yet will I remember the covenant I made with you in the days of your youth, and I will establish an everlasting covenant with you" (Ezekiel

16:60). So enduring is the bridegroom's faithfulness that he promises to "make atonement for you for all you have done" (16:63). Care, hurt, anger, faithfulness — such words describe God's love for his people. Even through our unfaithfulness he remains true.

This is the kind of bridegroom we have. He never wavers in his devotion for us. "I have loved you with an everlasting love" (Jeremiah 31:3). He has laid down his life for us (Ephesians 5:25).

May our lives and marriages mirror this love, as we love God and one another. "My command is this," declares Jesus, "Love each other as I have loved you" (John 15:12). Although often lacking in today's notion of love and marriage, this self-sacrificing love is to be the basis of all Christian relationships. Especially marriage.

We have followed the lovers through their courtship, wedding, separation and reunion. Now we turn to the poem's final division. In the closing verses we'll get a final look at the main Song's participants: the beloved, the king, the friends and the brothers. Let's go with the lovers as they reminisce and reaffirm their love.

"Come away, my lover,
and be like a gazelle
or like a young stag
on the spice-laden mountains."

REMINISCENCES
SONG OF SONGS 8:5-14

Once again fragrant blossoms appear on tree and field. Another spring has arrived. A pair of gazelles darts across the mountainside.

Friends

> **5 Who is this coming up from the desert leaning on her lover?**

The final division of the Song opens as did the wedding scene (3:6): "Who is this coming up from the desert . . . ?" There the Shulammite had asked the question concerning Solomon's wedding procession. Here the friends apply it to the Shulammite. Previously the question had introduced the consummation of the love relationship. Now it introduces a more settled relationship.

That she is leaving "the desert" signifies that she is leaving behind her days of depression and sorrow. The excitement of courtship and the wedding are past. So is the grief of separation which opened the Song's previous section. We now see a more mature and contented woman walking with and leaning on her lover. Beside them walk their friends.

Not only does this verse introduce the final portion of the Song, it also introduces the most difficult. Commentators agree that "it is simply impossible to render an interpretation satisfactory in every respect, especially in matters of detail."[14] That may be true. But the mood of this section is unmistakable. It is restful and reflective. As the remaining verses speak of young love, it becomes clear what is taking place. The lovers are reminiscing. First, the Shulammite recalls the awakening of their love:

Beloved

> Under the apple tree I roused you;
>> there your mother conceived you,
>> there she who was in labor gave you birth.
> 6Place me like a seal over your heart,
>> like a seal over your arm;
> for love is as strong as death,
>> its jealousy unyielding as the grave.
> It burns like blazing fire,
>> like a mighty flame.
> 7Many waters cannot quench love;
>> rivers cannot wash it away.
> If one were to give
>> all the wealth of his house for love,
>> it would be utterly scorned.

In recalling the birth of their love, the beloved describes it as if the king first began to live when he met her. The Song has already related their meeting out in the country. Now the beloved adds the detail that it was under an apple tree.

Some see the apple tree as a reference to the tree of the knowledge of good and evil in the Garden of Eden (Genesis 2 & 3). There God's forgiving love was aroused when Adam and Eve ate of the forbidden fruit and fell into sin. There God made the first promise of the Savior who would die for sinful mankind. If, indeed, this is a reference to the events of Eden, it answers the age-old question of what kind of fruit they ate.

The beloved desires to be "like a seal" over her lover's heart and on his arm. The seal, bearing its owner's name, was used to make impressions in clay or other soft substances. It represented the owner's signature. Moreover, the seal symbolized confidence and support. For the lover to wear her seal would be akin to our exchange of rings — a symbol of mutual commitment and love.

"Love," she declares, "is as strong as death"! Just as death or the grave (Hebrew *sheol*; see the discussion of Ecclesiastes 9:10) will not give up the dead, love will not let go of the loved one. Notice that the beloved does not speak of *my* love or *your* love but simply *love*. She is speaking of the perfect love which only God can give.

The strength and constancy of this love is quite different from the love often exhibited between a man and a woman. What Martin Luther observed back in his day is often the case today, too. "I have observed many married couples coming together in such great passion that they were ready to devour each other for love, but after a half year the one ran away from the other."[15] God's love, however, is unyielding. Nothing can "separate us from the love of God that is in Christ Jesus our Lord" (Romans 8:39). This is why God calls Christian spouses to model their marriages on Christ's sacrificial love and not to build solely on human emotions.

The beloved clearly refers to divine love as she continues. "It burns like blazing fire, like a mighty flame." The last phrase is better translated, "like the very flame of the Lord." It's unfortunate that the NIV relegates the more accurate and powerful translation to a footnote. This is the only reference to God's name in the entire Song. In Ecclesiastes Solomon builds to a climax in the closing verses. Here he also saves the high point for his ending. Throughout the poem Solomon has been hinting at a love which transcends human love. Now he names the source of that love. It is the LORD (Hebrew *Yah*), who is always "abounding in love and faithfulness" (Exodus 34:6).

God's burning love for us is unquenchable. He has loved us to the point of sending his Son Jesus to die for us. He loves us so much that he gives us forgiveness and eternal life in heaven. In his love he showers us with blessings beyond measure and uses everything for our eternal good.

Such giving love cannot be bought or sold. This is true of love between a husband and wife, and all the more so of the love between God and his people. God's love comes to us as a free gift!

Friends

<blockquote>

⁸We have a young sister,
and her breasts are not yet grown.
What shall we do for our sister
for the day she is spoken for?
⁹If she is a wall,
we will build towers of silver on her.
If she is a door,
we will enclose her with panels of cedar.

</blockquote>

The friends who speak here are very likely the beloved's brothers. Earlier the poem had indicated that the beloved did not have any sisters (6:9). Who, then, is the "young sister"? It is probably the beloved herself.

Her brothers are recalling when she was a young woman. They point out their concern that she be kept pure "for the day she is spoken for." Perhaps it was this concern for her that led to their seemingly harsh treatment of the beloved, when they were angry with her and made her tend the vineyards (1:6). They wanted to keep her busy and out of trouble.

The brothers' question concerning their sister is that of every Christian family. They want to know what is best. They supply the answer to their own question. They will defend her. The "towers" represent defense. Silver towers symbolize beauty along with virtue and firmness. The "panels of cedar" also stand for beauty and defense. If she, like a door, is open to advances, the brothers will be strict and keep her in.

We find similar imagery in the prophets. In Jeremiah 1:18,19 God says he has fortified the Prophet Jeremiah: "I have made you a fortified city, an iron pillar and a bronze wall to stand against the whole land. . . . They will fight against you but will not overcome you, for I am with you and will rescue you."

The way to purity and strength is through the Word of God. We are surrounded by temptations and attacks upon our Christian faith. We are engaged in a spiritual struggle "against the powers of this dark world and against the spiritual forces of evil in the heavenly realms" (Ephesians 6:12). We need to read, study, think about and put into practice the truths of Scripture. In our day of spiritual indifference and moral breakdown we dare not be caught with our defenses down.

At times God uses afflictions to hem us in and keep us from going astray. Life's troubles help to keep us humble and teach us to rely more fully on the Lord and his promises.

But some might wonder, "What if I haven't kept myself pure? What if time and again I've given in to temptations instead of resisting them?" Then we are to remember God's grace. Jesus laid down his life for his bride, the church. "Christ loved the church and gave himself up for her to make her holy, cleansing her by the washing with water through the word, and to present her to himself as a radiant church, without stain or wrinkle or any other blemish, but holy and blameless" (Ephesians 5:25-27). In the cross of Christ we find forgiveness. Through the cleansing power of baptism, the "visible Word," we have received a fresh start for each new day.

Beloved

> [10]I am a wall,
> and my breasts are like towers.
> Thus I have become in his eyes
> like one bringing contentment.
> [11]Solomon had a vineyard in Baal Hamon;
> he let out his vineyard to tenants.
> Each was to bring for its fruit
> a thousand shekels of silver.
> [12]But my own vineyard is mine to give;
> the thousand shekels are for you, O Solomon,
> and two hundred are for those who tend its fruit.

The beloved replies that rather than being an open door she is a wall and tower. She has kept her love for her husband alone.

She goes on to say that she has become "like one bringing contentment." Here we have a play on words which is lost in the translation. She brings *shalom*, that is, peace or contentment. This word is related to the names Solomon and Shulammite (see 6:13). Solomon has brought her peace. Now she in turn is a bringer of peace.

This is the way it is with Christ and his church. He brings us peace with God. We are to bear that peace to all the world. The gospel is something that we need to receive before we can pass it on to others.

The mention of Solomon's name in verse 11 is the fifth in the poem (1:1; 3:7,9,11). The verse also contains the poem's fourth reference to vineyards (1:6; 2:15; 7:12). A check of the other passages shows that they were different vineyards. This one is Solomon's, and it is located in Baal Hamon. Although this site is mentioned nowhere else in the Bible, it does occur in the Apocrypha (Judith 8:3). It was possibly located in Samaria on Mt. Ephraim, about thirty miles north of Jerusalem. The name Baal Hamon means "lord of plenty" and calls to mind Solomon's wealth. The vineyard keepers were each to bring King Solomon a thousand shekels of silver (about twenty-five pounds).

The Prophet Isaiah builds on this picture of the lover's vineyard. "I will sing for the one I love a song about his vineyard: My loved one had a vineyard on a fertile hillside" (Isaiah 5:1). Isaiah proceeds to describe how the loved one cultivated and cared for the vineyard. "Then he looked for a crop of good grapes, but it yielded only bad fruit" (5:2). This vineyard, says Isaiah, belongs to the Lord and is "the house of Israel and the men of Judah" (5:7).

Building still further on the Song's picture, Jesus himself told two parables about vineyards. One tells of workers in the vineyard and how the landowner (representing God) chose to pay all the workers the same wage (Matthew 20:1-16). The other parable relates how some wicked tenants refused to pay the landowner (God) and even put his son (Jesus) to death (Matthew 21:33-45).

All these parables clearly draw their language from the Song of Songs. They also clearly represent God and his people. The Lord expects his people to work for him, and he looks for results from that work — "justice" and "righteousness" (Isaiah 5:7). We can never pay our Savior back for the eternal salvation he gives us. But we can serve him with our lives and our love.

After discussing Solomon's vineyard, the beloved talks about her own. Whether or not this is the same vineyard as in the Song's opening chapter, we aren't told. Nor does it really matter. The point she makes has little to do with the vineyard itself. Rather, she is expressing her love for her husband. A thousand shekels is the owner's share of the vineyard. She gives that all to her lover and keeps back only the bare essentials for the care of the vineyard.

This beautiful expression of selfless love is a model for every marriage and moves us to think not of ourselves first, but of our partner's needs.

This is also a beautiful model for Christians in general. Everything we have really belongs to God. Let's not hold back from the good Lord who has so richly blessed us. "Whatever you do," urges the Apostle Paul, "do it all for the glory of God" (1 Corinthians 10:31).

Lover

> ¹³**You who dwell in the gardens**
> **with friends in attendance,**
> **let me hear your voice!**

Beloved

> ¹⁴**Come away, my lover,**
> **and be like a gazelle**
> **or like a young stag**
> **on the spice-laden mountains.**

We have come to the Song's closing exchange between Solomon and the Shulammite. The king harks back to their days of courtship (2:14). Again he longs to hear her voice.

The friends of whom Solomon speaks are male, another hint at a meaning beyond the superficial.

While the king longs to hear his beloved's voice, her longing is to see him. She desires to see him running gracefully on the spice-laden mountains like a gazelle or young stag. No doubt she pictures herself at his side.

Once more the setting is exotic, as it has been throughout this magnificent poem. We have followed the loving couple through scenes replete with all kinds of animals and plants, vineyards and gardens, mountains and deserts, towers, armies, banquets and majestic processions. We have traveled from Jerusalem to Tirzah, from En Gedi to Lebanon. We have followed the lovers from the beginning of their courtship to their wedding day, from their separation and reunion to times of peaceful reflections.

That the poem's closing verse should be spoken by the beloved is only fitting. The Song is Solomon's. But his bride's words comprise half-again as many verses as do his words. The poem has largely been her song of love to him. It is also in keeping with the mood of the Song that at poem's end we find ourselves on the beautiful mountains of the north country and watching the graceful gazelle.

The poem has told the story of love between a man and a woman. It has served as a model for Christian love and marriage. But like that gazelle springing across the pages of the poem, there is an elusive quality to the Song of Songs. No matter how intently we study the book, it leaves us with a desire for more. We see glimpses of another love which doesn't fade with the passing of countless springtimes. Yet no sooner do we catch a glimpse of that other love but it has vanished. We want to capture, hold and examine it. As we have seen, however, the fuller unfolding of this theme God leaves to other portions of his Word.

There the bridegroom says to us, "Let me hear your voice!" "Call upon me in the day of trouble," he invites us, "and I will deliver you" (Psalm 50:15). "Lift up your voice with a shout, lift it up, do not be afraid, say . . . , 'Here is your God!' " (Isaiah 40:9). He wants to hear us talk to him — in bad times and in good. He wants to hear that we believe in him and love him and are proud of him.

"I have loved you with an everlasting love," declares the bridegroom. How shall we answer him? His dazzling wedding clothes still bear the stain of blood. He has given us his life. He has given us his love. He has brought us joy from heaven above.

"You are my love, my life, my all," our hearts reply, while our eyes gaze at that land of love and peace.

In the distance we watch two gazelles; they seem to float across the flowery fragrant mountains and then vanish.

Solomon's Song of Songs has come to an end.

NOTES ON ECCLESIASTES

[1] Paul E. Kretzmann, *Popular Commentary of the Bible* (St. Louis: Concordia, 1924), Vol. II, p. 263.

[2] Martin Luther, *Notes on Ecclesiastes*, in *Luther's Works*, ed. Jaroslav Pelikan (St. Louis: Concordia, 1972), Vol. 15, p. 48.
Unless noted otherwise, subsequent Luther quotes are from this commentary.

[3] Victor E. Richert and A. Cohen, *Ecclesiastes*, in *The Five Megilloth*, ed. A. Cohen (London: Soncino, 1952), p. 123.

[4] *Ibid.*

[5] Franz Delitzsch, *The Book of Ecclesiastes*, trans. M. G. Easton, *Commentary on the Old Testament in Ten Volumes* (Grand Rapids: Eerdmans, 1975), Vol. VI, p. 257.

[6] Ernest W. Hengstenberg, *A Commentary on Ecclesiastes* (Sovereign Grace Publishers, 1960), p. 126.

[7] F. C. Cook, *Ecclesiastes*, in *The Bible Commentary* (Grand Rapids: Baker, 1953), p. 99.

[8] Martin Luther, *What Luther Says*, ed. Ewald M. Plass (St. Louis: Concordia, 1959), Vol. III, pp. 1494-1495.

[9] G. Wolff, "The Eternal God Is Our Refuge: A Brief Commentary on Ecclesiastes," trans. John Sullivan, in *Wisconsin Lutheran Quarterly* (1982), Vol. 79, no. 1, p. 26.

[10] William Green, quoted by Josh McDowell, *Evidence That Demands a Verdict* (San Bernadino: Campus Crusade for Christ, 1972), p. 59.

[11] Dennis R. Getto, "Anxiety: Millions are tormented by this disorder," *The Milwaukee Journal*, December 10, 1984.

[12] Robert Gordis, *Koheleth, the Man and His World* (New York: Schocken Books, 1968), p. 301.

[13] Alexander Heidel, *The Gilgamesh Epic and Old Testament Parallels* (Chicago: University of Chicago Press, 1946), p. 70.

[14] Delitzsch, *Ecclesiastes*, p. 370.

[15] Hengstenberg, *Ecclesiastes*, p. 246.

[16] Herbert Carl Leupold, *Exposition of Ecclesiastes* (Grand Rapids: Baker, 1981), p. 287.

[17] Luther, *What Luther Says*, Vol. I, p. 112.

NOTES ON THE SONG OF SONGS

[1] Marvin H. Pope, *Song of Songs*, from *The Anchor Bible* (Garden City NY: Doubleday, 1977), p. 89.

[2] Franz Delitzsch, *The Song of Songs*, trans. M. G. Easton, *Commentary on the Old Testament in Ten Volumes* (Grand Rapids: Eerdmans, 1975), Vol. VI, p. 1.

[3] S. Craig Glickman, *A Song for Lovers* (Downers Grove IL: InterVarsity Press, 1976), pp. 30,31.

[4] Earlier editions of the New International Version attribute this entire passage (1:8-11) to the lover. The newest edition (1984) attributes verse 8 to the friends.

[5] Robert Gordis, *The Song of Songs* (New York: Bloch Publishing Co., 1954), p. 30.

[6] Fred Wight, *Manners and Customs of Bible Lands* (Chicago: Moody, 1953), pp. 131-133.

[7] *Ibid.*, p. 130.

[8] *Ibid.*

[9] Glickman, *A Song for Lovers*, p. 63.

[10] G. Lloyd Carr, *The Song of Solomon* (Downers Grove: InterVarsity Press, 1984), pp. 148,149.

[11] Earlier editions of the New International Version attribute this entire passage (6:10-12) to the lover. The newest edition (1984) attributes verse 10 to the friends. As my commentary indicates, I feel verses 11,12 are spoken by the beloved.

[12] Glickman, *A Song for Lovers*, p. 89

[13] Delitzsch, *The Song of Songs*, p. 140.

[14] H. Speckhard, "Summary Interpretation of the Song of Solomn," trans. Paul W. Ludwig, in *Wisconsin Lutheran Quarterly* (1966), Vol. 63, no. 3, p. 215.

[15] Martin Luther, *What Luther Says*, ed. Ewald M. Plass (St. Louis: Concordia, 1959), Vol. II, p. 899.

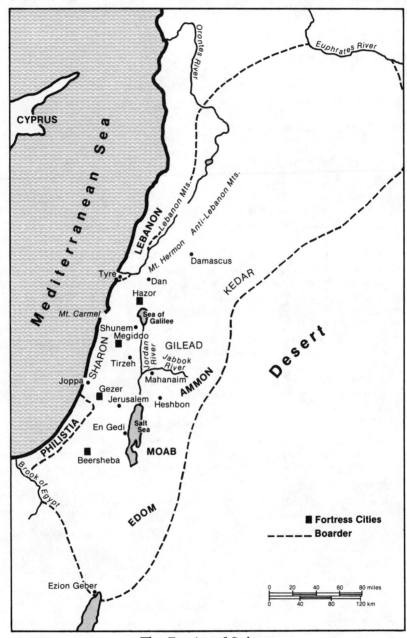

The Empire of Solomon